THE GREAT MARS HILL BANK ROBBERY

Center Point
Large Print

Books are produced in the United States using U.S.-based materials

Books are printed using a revolutionary new process called THINKtech™ that lowers energy usage by 70% and increases overall quality

Books are durable and flexible because of smythe-sewing

Paper is sourced using environmentally responsible foresting methods and the paper is acid-free

This Large Print Book carries the Seal of Approval of N.A.V.H.

THE GREAT MARS HILL BANK ROBBERY

Ron Chase

CENTER POINT LARGE PRINT
THORNDIKE, MAINE

This Center Point Large Print edition is published in the year 2017 by arrangement with Down East Books, an imprint of The Rowman & Littlefield Publishing Group.

Copyright © 2016 by Ronald D. Chase

The text of this Large Print edition is unabridged. In other aspects, this book may vary from the original edition. Printed in the United States of America on permanent paper. Set in 16-point Times New Roman type.

ISBN: 978-1-68324-470-7

Library of Congress Cataloging-in-Publication Data

Names: Chase, Ronald, 1947– author.
Title: The Great Mars Hill bank robbery / Ron Chase.
Description: Center Point Large Print edition. | Thorndike, Maine : Center Point Large Print, [2017] | Originally published: Camden, Maine : Down East Books, 2016.
Identifiers: LCCN 2017019756 | ISBN 9781683244707 (hardcover : alk. paper)
Subjects: LCSH: Bank robberies—Maine—Mars Hill—History. | Large print type books.
Classification: LCC HV6661.M22 C43 2017 | DDC 364.15/52092—dc23
LC record available at https://lccn.loc.gov/2017019756

To
Nancy, Eric, Adam, Hannah, and Raina

And in memory of
PFC Guy "Beanie" R. Bean
Died February 23, 1968
Quang Tri Province, Vietnam
Age 21
A friend

Contents

Prologue

I first learned of Bernard Patterson and the Mars Hill bank robbery while reading a series of three newspaper articles in the *Bangor Daily News* during the fall of 1973. His story immediately captured my interest. At the time, I was living in a rented mobile home in Calais, Maine, with my wife and infant son. My career with the Internal Revenue Service had just begun and we were barely subsisting on my sixty-five hundred dollar per year salary. The fascinating, dramatic yet often humorous tale about a fearless former Vietnam War hero turned improbable bank robber, who miraculously escaped to experience a succession of riotous intercontinental escapades while on the lam for nearly seven months was simply unbelievable. I remember thinking his story would rival the most exciting, compelling adventure novel. He seemed to be a real-life version of Don Quixote, Butch Cassidy and Robin Hood all rolled into one implausible package.

In truth, I related to him; and with some reservations, admired him. Both born in 1947, we grew up in working class families in rural Maine communities. Both of us had checkered, generally

9

unsatisfactory public school experiences and ended up in the army as nineteen-year-olds during the peak of the Vietnam War. At that juncture, our paths varied. Bernard was sent directly into the maelstrom of Vietnam where he experienced several years of combat, while mine was a much more benign exposure with tours of duty in Korea and Alaska. However, like hundreds of thousands of other young men who served during the Vietnam era, we both returned disillusioned, distrustful of our government institutions and with an abiding sense that we no longer fit neatly into the society we had left. His madcap, anti-establishment, albeit criminal, actions seemed to speak for all of us. There appeared to be some convoluted nuance of justice in his escape, the unrestrained, extravagant spending and casual, devil may care approach to the entire process.

I never forgot Bernard's adventures. An inveterate storyteller, whenever I travelled through Mars Hill on my way to or from an outdoor expedition in northern Maine or eastern Quebec, I invariably related the unbelievable events of his story to my usually doubtful companions. That I'm occasionally prone to embellishing a good story may have contributed to their skepticism. A companion on some of my canoe trips in northern Maine and a frequent victim of my story telling, my youngest son Adam may know the facts as I used to relate them almost as well as I. Perhaps the most remarkable aspect of this tale is that the facts are so incredible they eliminate any need for embellishment.

In January 2013, while on a winter mountaineering trip in New Hampshire, I had a fortuitous encounter with Peter King. Overhearing him talking with a companion about a fellow he had worked with who had robbed a bank in northern Maine and was "the most reckless person" he'd ever met immediately caught my attention. Striking up a conversation, I asked if the bank he'd robbed had been in Mars Hill. Affirming that it was, we had an extended conversation about his experiences working and socializing with Bernard. Before it ended, I announced my intent to write a book about him and the robbery.

Peter ended our conversation by stating that he liked and admired Bernard and counted him as a friend. That was an observation that has been regularly repeated by virtually everyone that I've interviewed who knew him intimately. Bernard was a good and loyal friend who engendered that same fidelity in people who befriended him. He was exceedingly likeable, humorous in a caustically sarcastic manner and despite his actions and behavior perceived to be a "good guy." When I first contacted one lifelong friend, his initial response was that he would not be party to anything that degraded Bernard. As much as a half century later people who knew him invariably say, "Bernard was a friend."

The late sixties and early seventies was a turbulent period for many in America, but probably none more than returning combat veterans. Dramatic social change rapidly evolving in a constricted timeframe, it was punctuated by strident sometimes violent disagreement over the moral acceptability and strategic value of the Vietnam War. Antiwar sentiment dominated the social and political landscape. Barely men, thousands of rural Maine teenagers like Bernard who entered the service in the mid-sixties left a sheltered world of school dances, conservative values and relatively secure circumstances; although the latter was not true of Bernard. Only the most daring among them had experimented with alcohol or dabbled in sex; and marijuana use was almost nonexistent.

While in the military, particularly Vietnam, many were exposed to a world of hard drugs, pervasive prostitution, corruption, desperate poverty and incomprehensible violence. Bernard experienced all of these in the extreme. However, unlike veterans from previous wars, Vietnam War returnees encountered a very different environment than the one they left; one of changing mores, heavy drug use and hostility toward veterans. Resentments, antisocial behavior and adaptability problems on the part of many veterans often resulted.

The Vietnam War was also unique in recent American history as it was a class war. World War II had been fought by a cross section of young men from all segments of society. This was also true of the Korean War, although to a somewhat lesser extent. For most of the Vietnam War, student draft deferments had the effect of exempting much of the middle and upper classes from service. Although there are no definitively reliable statistics, it's generally accepted that in excess of seventy-five percent of the enlisted men who served in Vietnam were from working class or poverty level backgrounds and that only about ten percent of the young men who came of draft age during the Vietnam War actually served in the military. This too fueled resentment among many Vietnam era veterans. By all accounts, Bernard came from financially poor circumstances. It's not surprising that the justification he used for robbing the bank was to forcibly take out a loan after he was reputedly denied college education benefits by the Veteran's Administration. He had been promised education benefits and he believed he was entitled to them. Frustrated, he took action.

Bernard was a genuine war hero. From 1966 to 1970, he served with the 25th Infantry Division in the Cu Chi sector of Vietnam and then the 101st Airborne near Hue. Only required to complete a one year term, he volunteered for two additional tours. Several accounts indicate that his request to volunteer for a fourth tour was denied based on concerns about the state of his mental health. Perhaps the symptoms of post-traumatic stress disorder (PTSD) had already manifested themselves.

An infantryman, he volunteered as a "tunnel rat," probably the most dangerous military assignment in the Vietnam War. Given the attenuated nature of the tunnel complexes, tunnel rats were invariably small in stature. Bernard was five feet three inches tall and weighed about one hundred and forty pounds. A lifelong friend described him as, "brazen and brave. He was a small guy but you instinctively knew, don't mess with him."

Bernard was also utilized as an enemy tracker above ground. Another very hazardous duty, he and his well-trained "tracker dog" would be air lifted by helicopter to an area the Viet Cong was suspected to inhabit. If the enemy was located, he would radio the helicopter to pick him and the dog up before the area was targeted with heavy ordnance. The tracker dogs were so valued he speculated that the army was more concerned about the dog's safety than his.

Bernard excelled in this violent, perilous world. A friend who encountered him at Camp

Eagle in Vietnam characterized Bernard as quiet, laid back and easy going but fearless. And, after his military service, he just didn't care. While one family member states that Bernard emphatically denied any PTSD problems, it seems quite likely that PTSD played a significant role in his decisions and behavior after leaving the military. One expert with a background dealing with combat veterans indicates that his was classic PTSD behavior.

Regardless of the motivations, Bernard's was an epic journey and a story worth telling.

• 1 •

Reflections

"(Bernard) could learn more in two days than the rest could in a week."
—A teacher

More than thirty-five years later, he could still vividly remember those harrowing episodes in the tunnels of Cu Chi. Silently crawling in the dark, trying to regulate and muffle his breathing, all of his senses in a state of extreme, hyper vigilance. Perspiring profusely in the steamy filth, beads of sweat filling and partially blinding his eyes, the ghastly foul, nauseating smell permeating the thin air, he inched his way through the narrow tunnels. Flicking his flashlight on and off as he crawled through mud in search of signs of booby traps while carrying a thirty-eight caliber revolver in his other hand and a bayonet strapped to his leg. The enemy was somewhere ahead of him. Maybe waiting in ambush or if he was lucky and sufficiently wily, he'd be undetected and surprise them. Either way, it was kill or be killed. There were no second chances in that hellish subterranean world of unyielding, appalling rules. Perpetually calm and unafraid, he'd always been the killer. Bernard had been one of the few tunnel rats to survive unscathed; at least physically.

At age fifty-six, Bernard Patterson was still relatively young. Living in a recently built home on Young Lake Road in Westfield, Maine, with his youthful fiancé and their infant daughter, life for him was in renewal. His had been a circuitous odyssey that had begun just a few miles away in Presque Isle on January 14, 1947. An inauspicious and anonymous beginning, few would have predicted the improbable events that defined his life.

During the warm summer days of 2003, his health was waning. Still regularly using marijuana and chain smoking unfiltered Pall Malls, Bernard reflected back on his exceptional life. Having remarked several times to friends that a book should have been written about him or even better a movie made, he'd tried to sell his story but couldn't get anyone to commit to serious money. Incessantly calculating the best possible option in all aspects of life and convinced he had a valuable commodity with which to bargain, he refused to sell his story cheap. Unfortunately for him, there had been no enthusiastic well-heeled writers or movie makers to come forward with a lucrative proposal.

Born into a poor family, childhood friends and

acquaintances remember him as reticent, unobtrusive, and likeable. He was quiet with people he didn't know but he was personable with friends. Girls liked him. Two attributes stood out; he was fearless and very intelligent. Although he was a little guy, it was universally understood, even at an early age; Bernard was no one to mess with. Dysfunctional would aptly characterize Bernard's childhood. As one friend succinctly put it, "he lacked good role models." His father was an intermittent laborer and his mother worked odd jobs when she was emotionally able and opportunity availed. Struggling with mental illness throughout much of her life, Glenna Patterson signed herself into the Bangor Mental Health Institute on several occasions when coping was no longer an option. Bernard had three brothers and two sisters.

Mars Hill potato farmer Duane Grass remembers him, his brother Bobby and mother picking potatoes in their family fields for many years when Bernard was a kid. During that era, it was common for whole families to pick potatoes. For many, the potato-picking income was an essential part of their sustenance used to buy clothes or pay for other necessary living expenses. Or the money would be set aside as a safeguard against possible emergencies during the upcoming long, cold northern Maine winter. The Patterson family lived hand-to-mouth and immediately used any income for their daily wants and needs. Money left over for a rainy day was a luxury for only the more fortunate to contemplate, never an alternative for them.

While potato picking was an integral part of northern Maine culture during his youth, it was rugged, demanding work. Up at four in the morning, potato trucks would gather pickers between 5:00 and 5:30 a.m. Always dark and usually cool, if not cold—unless workers were favored enough to get one of the treasured spots in a heated cab with the driver—they had a very chilly trip standing on an open platform in the back of the truck. Holding onto barrels or ropes secured to the truck bed, it was a dusty, windy ride to the fields. Swallowing blowing dirt and eyes filled with grit was an occupational hazard that finally ended when work began, unless it was a windy day.

If the truck didn't break down, which frequently happened, picking generally started at six in the morning. Seasoned pickers stood bending into their work. The inexperienced and many children knelt, paying a painful price as the often frozen ground rubbed skin off their knees. The choice was a persistently sore back or raw, bloodied knees. Veteran field hands understood that while kneeling minimized back pain, it was less efficient and guaranteed a poor paycheck. Days often began with frigid temperatures and sometimes ended as warm as eighty degrees. Heavily dressed for the morning cold, the insulated clothing resulted in unpleasant overheating if there was a warm afternoon sun.

After the first few days of harvest season, clothing degenerated. Gloves developed holes in the tips. Exposed fingersgrew numb from frost or bruised by rocks furtively concealed in the assigned potato rows. Pants and shoes dedicated to picking were caked with dirt and stank with the smell of rotten potatoes. On blustery days, wind usually blew from the northwest gusting down across the fields, forcing thick, sticky dust into the nose, eyes, mouth, and any openings in the picker's clothes. The ubiquitous bandanna wrapped tightly around the picker's face only provided marginal protection. Bernard habitually wore a navy blue bandanna given to him by his mother. If it rained or snow fell after the potatoes had been overturned, the field needed to be picked clean irrespective of the inclement weather.

Micmac baskets were used to gather the potatoes and then carried to a barrel. Once filled, the barrel was ticketed with the picker's card-stock number and the process began again. The most industrious laborers would fill a hundred or more barrels in a day and were paid twenty-five cents a barrel. Weary bones, parched faces, dirty bodies, big appetites, and a few needed dollars was the end result of a hard day's work in the fields. In many respects, Bernard was weaned and toughened by that rigorous austere environment.

At the time, numerous families in the area were poor but the Patterson family was more destitute than most. The late Northern National Bank teller, Ola Orser, recollected that Bernard frequently accompanied his mother into the bank when she cashed their potato-picking paychecks. In his youth, money always came hard for Bernard. Beginning at an early age, he learned that the bank on Main Street in Mars Hill was where one went to get needed cash.

The first recollections that Doug Pierce had of Bernard was when they were in the second grade. Doug was much taller and stronger, while Bernard was small and wiry. The two got into a wrestling match the first time they met. Doug having successfully twisted Bernard's arm behind his back, Bernard did a complete somersault to escape the hold. Surprise and innovation were intuitive traits that Bernard possessed and effectively utilized throughout his life.

Recalling that he was really tough and nimble, Pierce was one of his regular chums during grade school. When they played backyard football, Bernard was a real scrapper and one of the fastest runners. Crafty and sneaky, he was a bit of a loner.

In the late 1950s, the Patterson family home located at the top of York Street in Mars Hill was lost to a devastating fire. This would be the first of several fires that would impact his life. With no place to live, the family split up and moved in various directions; the children were sent to homes that would take them in. His older brother George looked out for him and his siblings to the extent his limited means allowed. Bernard also lived sporadically with his uncle, Grover Patterson, in the adjacent community of Blaine for many years. Bernard "lacked solid footing" a close friend regretfully observed.

Years later, in a rare sentimental moment, Bernard would share the painful disappointment he felt with the absence of his mother for much of his youth. While he had outwardly accepted his childhood predicament with a stern uncompromising stoicism, he expressed a deep inner resentment at being farmed out to multiple, sometimes unwilling, family members as a kid. In Bernard's unforgiving world, there was little space for inner contentment.

"He pretty much raised himself," observed frequent teenage companion, Larry Donovan. "Bernard often didn't know if he had a place to sleep or not." Larry's father and sister would have a very unique and frightening encounter with Bernard a few years later.

Larry and Bernard worked together in the potato houses after school and on weekends. Grimy, strenuous work, it was an assembly line process with the potatoes shoveled into barrels, loaded on conveyor belts, sorted for quality, back onto belts, and then stuffed into fifty and 100-pound burlap bags that were stitched closed. The heavy sealed bags were loaded on trains and trucks. The dirtiest, lowest position in the line was down in the hole shoveling potatoes and the worst job in the hole was emptying out rotten potatoes. The male workers periodically switched jobs so that all were relegated to time in the hole. Weighing in at a mere 120 pounds, Bernard hardened mentally and physically with the exhausting work. Paid ten dollars a day for his labors, that was big bucks in the early 1960s.

Too poor to participate in organized sports, Bernard began working at an early age. When not laboring in the potato fields and houses, he cut wood in the forest and split firewood for kindling. Having his own money was very important to Bernard, providing independence and self-esteem. He started smoking cigarettes and drinking beer in his early teenage years. A habit he regularly indulged later in life, marijuana was nonexistent in northern Maine during that time.

When not working, Bernard and his friends were frequently involved in minor delinquent behavior. In a prophetic portend of the future, he often carried a Bowie knife strapped to his leg. Cutting the loaded clotheslines of unsuspecting homemakers was just one of the activities he mischievously enjoyed with his unconventional toy. Larry remembers that he was not afraid of anybody or anything, but he was not a bully. As a teenager, he was reckless and unconcerned about consequences. When not misbehaving, they sometimes played basketball on the out-door court at Harry Orser's house, even on the coldest winter days.

Quiet in school, Bernard wasn't involved in formal extracurricular activities and didn't stand out. Although far from an academic, he excelled in studies when inclined. Attending Central Aroostook High School in Mars Hill, he didn't graduate. His high school principal, William Yersa, remembered that Bernard was in the class of 1967 but only for one and a half years. Yersa discerned, "He had a lot on the ball, there was no question about it." Another teacher nostalgically opined, "[Bernard] could learn more in two days than the rest could in a week."

According to Larry Donovan, "He had a very bad attitude about school. He was too bright, bored with everything. He was bored with life; he had a high IQ but not stimulated by school." Bernard left high school during his sophomore year in 1965.

In early 1966, Bernard joined the army. The Vietnam War was beginning to escalate. After boot camp and advanced infantry training, he was sent directly to Vietnam like thousands of his peers. Nineteen-year-old Private Patterson was assigned to the 25th Infantry Division which was located in Cu Chi Province about twenty-five miles northwest of Saigon.

The Cu Chi sector contained a vast tunnel network used by the Viet Cong for concealment. The tunnels were of great significance to the Viet Cong war effort and a major military obstacle for American forces. Not only was the enemy able to hide in them during the day only to steal out and attack at night, but they served as storage areas for supplies and ammunition. Larger more elaborate complexes were used as living quarters for companies of Viet Cong and temporary homes for North Vietnamese Army infiltrators. In 1966, U.S. troops conducted a major campaign, Operation Crimp, to destroy the Cu Chi tunnel system. Although it caused an immense amount of destruction to the jungle and terrain above ground, the effort essentially failed.

By the time Bernard arrived, the Allied Forces had adopted a new tactic and had begun training a courageous elite corps of men in tunnel warfare known as "tunnel rats." Tunnel rats were an all-volunteer force and for reasons known only to him, Bernard volunteered. And he kept volunteering. The normal tour of duty in Vietnam was twelve months but he volunteered for an additional two years and was denied a request for another.

Tunnel rats were a select cadre of mentally and physically tough, daring volunteers who were sent into the extensive, elaborate underground tunnel systems created by the Viet Cong. Their mission was simple, brutal, and extremely hazardous. Kill the enemy and destroy their tunnels with explosives. Their motto was *"Non gratum anus rodentum,"* literally Latin for "Not worth a rat's ass."

The Cu Chi sector had the most substantial tunnel system in Vietnam. When a tunnel complex was located, tunnel rats were lowered into narrow holes in the ground to seek out the enemy. These attenuated tunnels traveled deep into the ground for hundreds of yards or more to lower levels where larger more sophisticated facilities existed. While they provided a crude, extremely unpleasant existence for the inhabitants, they were the backbone of the Viet Cong resistance. Some of these underground fortifications were over twenty years old and often contained barracks for company size units or larger, training areas, storage facilities, and more. Hospitals and entertainment rooms were built into the tunnel system and there was one instance when comedian Bob Hope and his troupe were entertaining soldiers in the Cu Chi Base Camp while Viet Cong entertainers were simultaneously performing in a tunnel directly under them. On another occasion, an American tank was stolen, buried, and then used as an underground Viet Cong command post. Usually equipped with only a pistol, bayonet, and a flashlight, tunnel rats frequently entered this dank, murky, hellish world alone in search of the Viet Cong.

Infested with booby traps and the enemy often waiting in ambush, the tunnels were perilous in the extreme. Sometimes they encountered poison gas. A few tunnel rats wore gas masks but many entered without them as the masks impeded breathing, visibility, and their ability to hear—senses essential to survival. Booby traps could consist of sophisticated small explosives or something as rudimentary as well-placed bamboo lances designed to impale those unaware of their existence. Other creatures haunted the tunnels such as snakes, rats, and scorpions. Venomous snakes and rats infected with the bubonic plague were sometimes left as living booby traps. Water traps were U-shaped dips built into the tunnel complex to prevent the injection of tear gas into the system. When encountered they required tunnel rats to submerge and swim to the other side, gambling that they'd find nothing but putrid air when and if they emerged. A combination of human waste, rotting food, and sometimes decaying bodies created incredibly revolting, fetid conditions in the tunnels.

Only a handful of soldiers had the unique blend of courage, intelligence and command of their emotions to survive and excel as a tunnel rat. They were the antithesis of the modern American soldier with high-tech weaponry, mechanized armament, artillery backup, and readily available air support. A throwback to a different time, they faced the enemy one on one while possessing only the basic tools of combat without support. A rat's knife and handgun were his best friends. The psychological and physical demands were enormous. Crawling for hundreds of yards in pitch black, narrow tunnels where the pervasive threat of death or severe injury existed; being buried alive was a constant fear. Just a few could cope with the claustrophobia, and only about one in ten were able to complete the specialized training that consisted of simulated conditions. The result was an exclusive esprit de corps among the tunnel rats. Modern-day samurai, they knew they were exceptional warriors enviously viewed by others as heroes that were a bit unhinged.

Life as a tunnel rat was an extremely dangerous existence with a very high casualty rate. Bernard excelled in his new occupation and subsequent assignment as a solo reconnaissance specialist with the 101st Airborne Division, seeking out the enemy above ground in the jungle with a tracker dog. His keen intellect, calm demeanor, and fearlessness served him well. Awarded four Bronze Stars for valor including one for taking command of a platoon in combat, four Commendation Medals, the Air Medal, and nominated for the Silver Star, the much decorated hero quickly rose to the rank of sergeant.

These and many other memories were undoubtedly part of his consciousness during the summer of 2003. Vietnam had been but one violent chapter in his adventurous life. Returning a hero to an unappreciative country, he conducted one of the most daring, spectacular bank robberies in the history of the State of Maine, managed a miraculous escape, and lived out an implausible succession of wild escapades that spanned three continents for more than seven months before he was captured and imprisoned. Returning to the area where he'd grown up after prison, he continued living life in the extreme; albeit not with the same reckless abandon of a bank robber. He'd learned how not to get caught, most of the time.

His perpetually active, exceptional mind bounded from one faraway memory to another. The house fire where much was lost and almost everything changed, the exhilarating sense of freedom he experienced horseback riding as a kid, the blinding flash and deafening echo of a gunshot intended for him in one of the tunnels of Cu Chi, picking potatoes with his brother on a cold fall day, stumbling through a snow-covered potato field dragging two water-soaked bags of stolen cash, draped over the humped back of a disagreeable camel staggering through the seemingly endless desert and numerous romances had and lost. These and many other recollections subliminally cluttered his consciousness.

Memories of the tunnels trumped all others. Looming just beneath the surface of his conscious mind, they were harsh ever-present companions.

• 2 •

Return Home

*"He was a very unhappy guy
when he didn't have money."*
                                    —A friend

Combat was just a part of the Vietnam experience for many American soldiers including Bernard. A subculture grew up around military bases and the servicemen that inhabited them, much of it negative. Prostitution, black markets, loan sharks, drugs, bars, and brothels were pervasive. Bernard was very much a part of that culture and later would often regale friends with graphic stories about whores, wild times, drinking, and drugs. He would nostalgically recall his hooch in Camp Eagle and the girls that catered to him.

A common practice for many soldiers was acquisition of a hooch, a small hut or room on or off base. Most had a mama-son: a Vietnamese girl who performed household chores, did other tasks like shining shoes, and laundry, sometimes providing sexual services. Unwittingly, Bernard and his peers were contributing to their own

31

vulnerability as most of the mama-sons were collaborating with the Viet Cong. Those that did not collaborate were summarily executed, often beheaded.

An extensive black market existed in Vietnam. Drugs were the most common, lucrative commodity but literally everything was bought and sold. Billions of dollars in food, equipment, armaments, medical supplies, and other goods shipped to Vietnam from the United States for the war effort never reached their intended destination. Often when these valuable commodities did filter down to the frontline soldier, the more daring, enterprising GIs would sell or barter the merchandise locally. Small fortunes were made by many soldiers, particularly officers and noncommissioned officers who had access to supplies and possessed the savviness needed to play that dangerous game. The risks were substantial dealing with Vietnamese and American cut-throats while enduring the ever-present danger of detection by military investigators and prosecution by an often harsh, excessively punitive judicial system. As in combat, Bernard was confident and unafraid.

Heavily involved in the black market, Bernard related the details of his illicit activities to many, and friends say that he always had an abundance of money while serving in the army.

The average monthly pay for a sergeant was about $250 yet he spent money extravagantly. One acquaintance commented that he "had an angle on everything."

Having an astute mathematical mind, Bernard developed a complex money-making scheme trading currencies in the black market. He would convert Vietnamese piasters to Military Pay Currency, then buy U.S. money orders and convert them back to piasters, sometimes making a 500 percent profit. When he was able to acquire much less easily obtainable American dollars, the sale of greenbacks was even more profitable. "He had great skills with numbers and had a scam for everything," according to his friend Mark Carney.

Utilizing his exceptional mental abilities and a sanguine brazen approach, Bernard educated himself on how to network in Vietnam and make money from a variety of sources. He accumulated knowledge and adroitness on how the supply system functioned and actively sold scarce American goods and military equipment to Vietnamese buyers at a substantial profit. Purchasing inexpensive widespread Vietnamese marijuana from indigent peasant farmers, he marketed this much sought after product to enthusiastic users in the military. After a life of poverty, Bernard finally had money to spare and he loved living the high life.

Prior to being permanently discharged from the service, Bernard returned home several times on extended leave from Vietnam. Normally, military leave would be granted for periods of two weeks to thirty days. He would return home for as long as he wanted, sometimes as much as fifty days at a time, invariably fortified with large amounts of cash. Having devised an elaborate scheme for smuggling marijuana home in his military baggage, he had an ample supply for both sale and to share with friends while on leave or AWOL. Profligate partying with alcohol, pot, and some harder drugs was the norm as he hung out with a group of friends, most of which were veterans.

When he ran out of money, Bernard returned to Vietnam. A contemporary friend remarked, "He was a very unhappy guy when he didn't have money." At least twice, Bernard was demoted because of long unapproved absences. However, the grade of sergeant was quickly reinstated as his combat services in that capacity were deemed invaluable.

Purchasing a new Corvette became an almost ritualistic routine when Bernard returned home from Vietnam on leave. Shortly after his arrival, he would visit Skip Carroll at Carroll's Auto Sales in Presque Isle and buy the sportiest Corvette Stingray on the lot even though he didn't have a driver's license. With an average cost in excess of $4,000, a Corvette was one of the most expensive automobiles of that generation. When he returned to Vietnam, Bernard gave them away.

Friends would willingly chauffeur Bernard both because they liked him and since he was the manna that nourished the party. On one occasion, he was out on his own driving at an excessive speed in his latest luxury sports car acquisition. Speed in anything propelled by a motor was a lifelong addiction. Spotted by local police, they gave chase but were left in the dust. When authorities finally located him and his gleaming new Corvette, Bernard was sitting in the passenger seat parked in a driveway, smiling. Brian Blanchard was at the wheel. Although convinced that Bernard had been the operator, the police were unable to ascertain who had been driving and no charges were brought. That both of them were servicemen who had recently returned from Vietnam probably played a role in that generous law enforcement decision.

Mark Carney was sixteen when he first recollects meeting Bernard. Because Bernard was a few years older, Mark didn't know him in school or growing up. Bernard was home on leave after a tour in Vietnam and already a local hero when they met at Ron & Fran's Diner in Mars Hill. Entertaining Mark with outrageous, unbelievable tales of life and combat in Vietnam, they became friends. Mark would follow in his footsteps and serve in Vietnam a few years later. There he would learn the often bitter, truthful reality of Bernard's once seemingly exaggerated stories.

In late 1970, Bernard finally separated from the army. He told several people that he had volunteered for an additional tour and his request was denied. The commonly held but uncorroborated belief is that the army determined that he lacked sufficient mental stability for retention. That he may have already exhibited symptoms of posttraumatic stress disorder is a distinct possibility. Regardless, people observed marked changes in his personality. A close friend recalls that, "(he) didn't care after the military." Another commented, "He went to Vietnam and came back crazy as a loon." Quite obviously, Bernard attempted to manage what-ever internal stress he had acquired from his Vietnam experiences with a steady diet of pot.

As in the past, Bernard returned from Vietnam flush with money. And he repeated his previous excesses of heavy drinking, pot smoking, and hard partying. Returning veterans provided him with a steady influx of fellow revelers that included many of the friends he served with in Vietnam. The normal pattern for the group was to meet at Al's Diner, a popular restaurant on Main Street in Mars Hill, a dry community at the time. There, evening plans were formulated, usually consisting of driving to bars in Presque Isle or more distant communities. On other occasions, they would simply agree to meet at a favorite rural location or someone's house to drink and smoke pot. Bernard didn't have a steady job. Having obtained a driver's license shortly after separating from the service, he quickly lost it due to reckless driving. Although he'd lost his license, he still had expensive cars and willing drivers if he didn't choose to drive himself.

In addition to hanging out with the usual gang, he began associating with a crowd known to be active in the local drug business. Stories abound of minor drug wars and disputes over drug debts. Two men, Gary Mahaney and David Bradbury, would later be convicted of murdering Brian Blanchard's brother Randy. A habitual pot smoker, Bernard needed a source after exhausting his stash smuggled home from Vietnam. Universally feared and respected by people on both sides of the law, those who knew him well assert that he was not prone to violence except to protect or avenge himself or his friends. He was considered by most to be a "good guy," albeit reckless and misguided.

Bernard was quickly running out of money and got involved in the sale of pot to support himself and his habit. Disposing of his flashy cars, he began using a borrowed Chevrolet Malibu for transportation. Although his financial dilemma prompted him to seriously consider the idea of selling his substantial combat skills as a mercenary soldier, he never actually followed up on the scheme in a meaningful way.

During the winter of 1970/1971, Bernard re-enrolled in high school with the intent of getting his high school diploma and going to college. He soon dropped out. Later, he would criticize the Veteran's Administration for failing to provide him promised assistance for his education. A common practice for recruiters and induction center employees during the Vietnam War era was to make exaggerated guarantees to young soldiers that the cost of their future education would be fully paid and they would receive free health care for life as rewards for honorable service. These were disingenuous commitments that were only partially true and couldn't realistically be kept. Bernard firmly believed that the government had failed to keep the many promises made to him and he was extremely resentful.

Now very low on cash, Bernard lacked a place to call home. Often using his Uncle Grover's residence in Bridgewater as something of a base camp, he moved around a lot. Reminiscent of his childhood, he often didn't know where he was going to sleep at night.

Somewhat uncharacteristically, in June 1971, he joined a friend for an extended backpacking trip in nearby Baxter State Park. The most spectacular mountain wilderness area in New England, they enjoyed several days hiking and camping in the Wassataquoik Lake region in the northern sector of the park. During that expedition, Bernard shared many of his most guarded inner secrets with his hiking companion and confidant.

Bernard became romantically involved in July and rented an apartment for the two of them on Academy Street in Presque Isle. Although seriously involved according to his unconventional definition of intimacy, he continued to see other women on the sly. In need of a reliable vehicle, he spent the last of his money buying a bright red Opel Kadett Coupe for the two of them to share. Fortunately, she had a license.

Money was a serious problem. In early August, he called Mark Carney and asked for a $50 loan. Mark agreed and drove to his apartment in Presque Isle to lend him the money. When he arrived, he found Bernard very intense and on edge. They went out to a local cafe for a beer. "(He was) very volatile, thought he might blow at any moment," Mark observed. Giving him the money, he knew something heavy was on Bernard's mind. Later in August,

Bernard and his girlfriend moved to an apartment on Jefferson Street in Bangor.

On August 14, 1971, Al's Diner was burglarized. The owner was Richard Carney, Mark Carney's uncle. A safe containing more than $1,600 was carried off. Later found empty in a nearby swamp, the door had been pried open and all of the money removed. Documents and other papers were scattered about. The following November, a grand jury would indict and order the arrest of David Bradbury for the burglary. Bernard was also charged with the same crime.

Bernard began routinely visiting the Northern National Bank branch in Mars Hill in early September. Entering the bank, he would sit in the lobby watching, observing, sometimes chatting with customers or employees. Often, he would call on the branch manager, Frank Brown, in his office. Bernard was there regularly and opened a safe deposit box, allowing him temporary surveillance of the interior of the bank vault. Observing the Brink's trucks making frequent deliveries and collections was one of the informed benefits of his careful inspections. As it was potato harvest season, the size and number of deliveries were more numerous than usual. When not in the bank, he would often sit at a soda fountain across the street in the Rexall Pharmacy carefully monitoring bank activities. No one considered his preoccupation with the bank unusual at the time.

Again desperate for money, Bernard called his longtime friend Brian Blanchard and asked for a $50 loan. Since Brian was gainfully employed, he had the cash and agreed. Bernard promised to repay the debt as soon as possible.

By late September, Bernard was broke again. Trying to maintain an apartment in Bangor, live the high life, and support his marijuana habit without income was an impossible task. After an argument with a friend, he left Bangor in the Opel Kaddett and drove to Blaine. Meeting a drinking buddy, they had several beers and concocted a plan to acquire some quick cash. Disguised with masks, they held up Smith's Truck Stop in Blaine getting away with about $3,000. After narrowly escaping, the two careless robbers drove to nearby Number 9 Lake and went fishing. Getting thoroughly drunk, they capsized their small boat, soaking themselves and the money.

Traveling back to Bangor that evening, when he arrived at his apartment Bernard unrolled a bundle of wet cash in front of an astonished group of friends and dried it on the kitchen table. Still intoxicated, he described the day's events in detail. They were reliable, trustworthy friends, no one ever ratted him out. Although Bernard became a suspect, law enforcement officers were unable to conclusively identify the robbers and the case was never solved.

Living extravagantly whenever he had money, it didn't take long for Bernard to exhaust the proceeds of the truck stop robbery. Soon, he was again looking for new sources of income. In late October, he and a friend left Bangor and drove to his grandmother's house in Bridgewater. Leaving his companion, he departed for an unidentified appointment. When he returned, he was furious, stating he had unfairly been denied a loan after providing the bank with years of business.

On the night of November 5, 1971, an abandoned barn on the Clark Road in Mars Hill burned to the ground. A spectacular fire, it lit up the nighttime sky and many in the community rushed to view it. Arson was suspected.

A large crowd also gathered on Main Street to watch the fire from a distance. Northern National Bank employees stepped outside the bank to get a better view. Bernard was among the crowd that night and observed that the bank vault was left wide open.

Later that evening, Bernard slowly drove down Mill Street adjacent to the potato houses and along the railroad tracks east of Main Street. Stopping opposite the potato houses at the end of Market Street in almost total darkness, he silently carried camping gear down the steep bank on the east side of the street and concealed it next to Prestile Stream.

For Bernard, everything he valued most was on the line; love, self-esteem, and well-being. He was out of money again and desperate.

• 3 •

The Robbery

"It was all part of a master plan,"
—Acting Police Chief Fay Fitzherbert

On the morning of November 12, Bernard arose early in his apartment on Jefferson Street in Bangor. Arranging a ride to the Broadway exit on Interstate 95, he hitchhiked to Blaine.

* * *

Located in the shadow of 1,748-foot Mars Hill Mountain in the heart of Aroostook County potato country with a population just under 1,900, Mars Hill was the quintessential small town America in 1971. Although the effects of the war in Vietnam, the political and social strife it spawned, and the drug culture of the late 1960s were beginning to impact the town, it was still very much a reflection of rural America: law abiding, church-going, and conservative. Potato was king. Children were recessed from school each fall to help harvest the potato crop. Most of the surrounding farms grew potatoes, and local businesses largely supported or existed for the potato industry.

Winter arrives early in northern Maine, and Friday evening November 12 was a cold, dark night with subfreezing temperatures. The streets and sidewalks were free of ice and snow, but there was a light blanket of snow in the surrounding fields. Ice was beginning to form along the shore of Prestile Stream, running north to south and paralleling the town on the east. Continuing past the southwestern end of Mars Hill Mountain, it flows for about seven miles through the Town of Blaine before entering New Brunswick, Canada.

In 1971, Main Street in Mars Hill, also U.S. Route 1, was an assortment of mid-twentieth century one- and two-story stores, eateries, and mom and pop service businesses. A wide street with diagonal parking on both sides, the sidewalks were immaculately maintained. Main Street was so broad cars would sometimes park in the middle of the road during busy periods creating an artificial median. A relaxed, uncomplicated thoroughfare, it was pristine, yet dusty given the heavy truck traffic.

The busiest time of year, potato harvest season, had just ended. The big event in Mars Hill that night was a school dance at the grade school gym. Eighth grader Stuart Craig vividly remembers attending the dance and the dramatic events that ensued.

A few minutes before 8:00 p.m., a woman called in a fire alarm to nurse Alice Morse at the Aroostook Health Center in Mars Hill. The regional medical facility handled calls for the volunteer Mars Hill Fire Department when no one answered the phone at the station. The report, a building was on fire on A.C.I. Street, nothing more. The caller then hung up. Morse turned in a fire alarm.

The three Mars Hill air horns systematically blared out a series of loud warnings alerting the entire community that there was a fire in the A.C.I. Street vicinity. The quiet, tiny Aroostook County hamlet of Mars Hill was now on high alert for a fire.

Townspeople were decidedly apprehensive about fires. In recent months, there had been an epidemic of potato house fires in the area and arson was believed to be the primary cause. The old potato houses were extremely flammable and a tempting target for arsonists. The tinder-box buildings caused huge, luminous fires that lit up the night sky in the evenings, and virtually the whole community would turn out to view the fireworks-like spectacles. This reported fire was the second in a week. On the previous Friday an old abandoned barn on the Clark Road belonging to Duane Grass had burned to the ground. Grass believed it was arson. The building had no electricity and there was nothing combustible in it.

* * *

Acting Police Chief Fay Fitzherbert, responsible for traffic control during a fire, was sitting in his cruiser at the Mobil Station facing York & Fenderson Hardware at the junction of Benjamin and Main streets when he first heard the fire alarms. The Mars Hill Police Department was a two-man force, but Chief James Crichton was incapacitated with shingles and other health problems. Fay Fitzherbert was the only law in Mars Hill that night.

Hearing the alarm, Fire Chief Normand McPherson drove to the fire station, located on the west side of upper Main Street between Benjamin and Silver streets, and organized an emergency response sending a fire truck driven by the same Duane Grass with a crew of volunteers to A.C.I. Street. By the time they passed Acting Chief Fitzherbert, a parade of vehicles was already pursuing the fire truck. He hurriedly followed in his cruiser. A quiet evening disrupted, shopkeepers and store goers were distracted and collectively concerned as the entourage sped south on Main Street with lights flashing and sirens screaming in search of a fire.

* * *

During the potato harvest season, abnormally large amounts of cash were generally kept on

47

deposit at the Northern National Bank. Many farmers compensated their potato pickers in cash. Whether by cash or check, they usually paid them on Friday or Saturday. With the harvest season winding down and holidays fast approaching, it was still a hectic, bustling time of year for local businesses, and most of their sales were in cash. The high volume of such transactions necessitated the bank maintaining a large cash reserve. A few days before, the bank had submitted an order for more cash, and Brink's had delivered on the requisition earlier in the day.

A one-story brick building, the bank was located on the east side of Main Street at the corner of Market Street, several hundred feet south of the Mobil Station where Acting Chief Fitzherbert was parked. Market Street dead ended at a long line of potato storage houses that paralleled Main Street about two hundred feet behind the bank. Railroad tracks, Mill Street, and a steep, densely wooded embankment that dropped precipitously to Prestile Stream were just beyond.

A rural bank in a low-crime environment, there were no alarms, guards, or cameras, and the bank vault, which was adjacent to the lobby on the left and otherwise unprotected, was sometimes left open. It was open that evening. With a total staff of five, a manager and four tellers, just two tellers were on duty that Friday night: Ola Orser and Rhona Sargent.

Matriarchal, white-haired, sixty-three-year-old Northern National Bank senior teller Ola Orser was wearily wrapping up her day that had been a protracted one. Friday was the longest and most frenzied workday of the week with numerous area workers cashing their paychecks, many arriving late in the day. Adding to the burden, a Brink's truck had delivered tens of thousands of dollars just a short time before. The bank had been short-handed for the past several hours as the two other tellers, Pearl Terrell and Martha Lawrence, and the bank manager, Frank Brown, had finished their shifts at 5:00 p.m. Her youthful co-worker, Rhona Sargent, age twenty-three, shared her fatigue. Closing time was only five minutes away.

According to bank policy, the tellers normally kept a limited amount of cash in their drawers, usually $1,500 or less. They also retained collected funds received during the day, safe-guarded in a small cabinet under their respective counters. All other monies were stored in a safe in the bank vault.

Co-owner of Bartley's Store in Blaine, Ella Bartley was standing to the right of the teller's counter in the bank lobby tallying up the day's business receipts for deposit. Burwell Donovan and his eleven-year-old daughter Launa walked

49

through the alcove, entered the bank, and turned to a high counter on their immediate left. As was their Friday night ritual, Donovan intended to cash his paycheck and then he and Launa, who worshiped her Dad and was almost always with him, would do the family grocery shopping.

With Launa standing close to him on his left, Donovan stepped to the counter to endorse his paycheck. At that moment a series of loud fire alarms captured the attention of those in the bank.

Outside, a drama was playing out just before closing time for Orser and Sargent. Distracted and curious, they wanted to know where the fire was, wondering and worrying whether it was their home or one belonging to someone they knew. The tellers glanced at their fire alarm chart. The pattern and number of alarms identified the presumed area of the fire to be A.C.I. Street. Regardless, three customers remained in the bank. They would have to be serviced before the tellers could close up shop and satisfy their curiosity.

* * *

Bernard was preposterously attired. A short man holding a soda carton in his right hand, he was carrying a large, awkward bundle wrapped under his left arm. He was clownishly dressed in a Marx Brother's style ankle-length dark trench coat and wearing a bushy, reddish brown wig.

His face was covered with his navy blue potato picking bandanna and oversized dark glasses that kept slipping down.

Trudging north on the east side of Main Street past Winnie's Restaurant, Bernard was intent on his destination, Northern National Bank. Despite his remarkably unusual costume, no one noticed him as he approached the bank on that cold, dark night. Blaring fire alarms distracted otherwise potential witnesses.

Closeted in his absurd costume, twenty-four-year-old Bernard counseled himself to relax and remain composed prior to entering the bank in much the same way he had done dozens of times before when crawling into the dangerous tunnels of Cu Chi. Reminding himself that this would be nothing compared to descending into a muddy, booby trap infested hole in the ground, with the Viet Cong waiting to kill or maim him, he pressed on. Like many occasions in the past, he was on a mission alone at night and unafraid. That's how he functioned best.

* * *

As Burwell Donovan turned away from the counter and headed toward his friend, head teller Ola Orser, Bernard abruptly burst from the darkness into the bank lobby. Accidentally shoving Launa against the counter with sufficient impact to hurt her ribcage, he directed the customers to look down at the floor. Also a decorated combat hero during World War II, Donovan calmly and protectively clasped his daughter's hand.

The three bewildered customers stared down at the floor in shocked disbelief as a ridiculously clad man brushed past them and approached teller Orser's window. At that very instant, the entire noisy fire procession, including Fire Chief McPherson and Acting Police Chief Fitzherbert, raced down Main Street past the bank en route to the presumed fire on A.C.I. Street.

Almost instantly recognizing young Bernard Patterson, Orser wondered why he was dressed in such an outlandishly silly outfit. She had known him since he was a little boy. Orser knew his distinct walk and obvious demeanor. She immediately discerned the disgustingly foul smelling cologne that both he and his brother persisted in wearing, which offended her acute sense of smell. She smiled as he approached.

When Bernard quietly announced he was holding up the bank, Orser grinned in disbelief, thinking it a joke. Unconvinced and doubting his intent, Orser wasn't taking him serious. Bernard persisted. Tiring of the presumed charade and desirous of finishing her workday, Orser told him that he'd carried the prank far enough and it was time for all of them to go home.

Frustrated, Bernard acrobatically leapt over the counter and screamed, "This is a holdup! Don't anybody move or push any buttons and you won't get hurt!" Removing a pistol from the soda carton, he menacingly pointed it at Orser's face. She would later relate, "I tried to remain calm and said a little prayer."

Worried about her weak heart, Bernard lowered the pistol, leaned forward and in a hushed voice informed her that the robbery was for real but reassured her she'd be safe. Bernard later told a friend, if Orser had said something assertive like "get out of here," he would have probably left. "He (Bernard) didn't have a mean bone in his body, he just wanted some money," his friend added.

Directing Sargent to join them, Bernard unrolled a large plastic garbage bag and a cloth laundry bag. Giving one to each teller, he ordered them filled with money. Frightened, they began apprehensively yet meticulously loading stacks of bills into the bags, most of it in small denominations.

Impatient with the tellers' tediously slow pace, Bernard put his pistol down on the floor and graphically instructed them on how to rapidly empty the cash drawers, haphazardly tossing bundles of money into the bags. Orser was momentarily tempted to grab the pistol but remembered it was contrary to bank policy to resist during a robbery, and Bernard's angry demeanor terrified her. Sargent would later comment that she considered kicking the pistol down the open cellar stairway but was too frightened to do so.

After their drawers and cabinets had been emptied of cash, Bernard directed the two tellers to finish filling the bags by removing money from the safe in the bank vault, which included the large Brink's deposit made just a short time before. The vault was outside of the teller's counter area to the left of the lobby and easily visible and accessible to the public when open.

Observing that the bank robber was preoccupied in the vault, Ella Bartley silently crept out the door. Once outside, she rushed into Newberry's Department Store in search of a phone to call the police. With a clerk's assistance, she found Chief Crichton's phone number and called him. Due to his health problems, he was unable to respond to the call with any personal action and couldn't reach Acting Chief Fitzherbert by phone. Fitzherbert was in his cruiser in search of a fire.

Desperate, Crichton called the home of Deputy Sheriff Edgar Wheeler in Bridgewater, a detective in the County Sheriff's Department. Reaching Wheeler's wife, Dottie, she called the Sheriff's Office who relayed a message by radio to Fitzherbert that the bank was being robbed. Deputy Wheeler was dispatched to the scene.

* * *

There was no fire on A.C.I. Street, just chaos. Fitzherbert, the fire department, and a mass of followers were confusedly searching in vain for a nonexistent fire. The traffic congestion hindered Fitzherbert's immediate departure but he was finally able to maneuver his vehicle free and rush to the bank. It was at that moment that Fitzherbert first realized that he and the entire community had been duped by what he perceived as an elaborate scheme. "It was all part of a master plan," he would later assert.

* * *

Both bags were filled with about fifty pounds of small denomination bills; the total amount Bernard had "withdrawn" was $110,248.96, the largest bank robbery in the history of the State of Maine. Politely thanking the tellers for their cooperation, Bernard nodded at the waiting customers and dragged the heavy bags of money across the lobby floor and disappeared into the night. The entire robbery had only taken about five minutes.

Bernard had experienced an incredible streak of good luck. His plan to the extent that he had one had worked to near perfection. An exceptionally large bank deposit had been made just before the robbery. No one had challenged him

55

with what he later stated was an unloaded pistol. No injuries or violence had occurred and now he was free with more than twenty-five times what he had earned during his entire tour in Vietnam. He stumbled and scrambled out into the darkness pulling his heavy burden while at least one bemused onlooker wondered what a strangely dressed man was doing leaving the bank with his laundry.

Moments later, Acting Chief Fitzherbert arrived at the scene. Approaching the bank, he noticed a gray Oldsmobile parked next to a garage opposite the bank on the corner of Market and Main streets. When he stopped in front of the bank, the Oldsmobile immediately sped off south on Route 1. An informant later told Fitzherbert that the occupants had a rifle pointed at him, and if he'd arrived prior to Bernard's departure, he would have been shot. Fitzherbert still believes that "missing him by twelve or thirteen seconds" saved his life. A frazzled Ola Orser greeted him at the bank door stating, "You just missed him."

Bernard was headed to a most implausible getaway vehicle.

• 4 •

The Search

"What happened, someone rob a bank?"
—A friend

After confirming that the robber had definitely left the building, Acting Chief Fitzherbert searched behind the bank on foot with a flashlight. Finding nothing, he returned to the cruiser and radioed the Aroostook County Sheriff's Office corroborating that a bank robbery had taken place. They in turn contacted the State Police in Houlton. In accordance with protocol for a bank robbery, a federal offense, the State Police notified the FBI.

Reentering the bank, Fitzherbert conducted a brief interrogation of the tellers and witnesses. Head Teller Ola Orser described the circumstances of the robbery and confided that she believed the thief, who was wearing a bushy red-haired wig, was Bernard Patterson, a young man she knew who had grown up in Mars Hill. Other witnesses provided somewhat conflicting descriptions. Customer Burwell Donovan recalled a man with curly, dark, chin level hair that was awfully dirty and untidy. Grocery store owner Ella Bartley remembered, "an artificial wig frosted or gray" and a "real gun." On one thing everyone agreed, he was dragging two large bags filled with money when he left.

Fitzherbert resumed his meticulous search for the robber in his cruiser. Using a large mounted spotlight, he drove down Mill Street around and between the potato storage houses behind the bank. Detecting no sign of anyone, he continued north to Main Street past the fire station and up Silver Street. Still finding no evidence of a man dragging two large bags of money or anything else suspicious, he back-tracked toward the bank.

Driving south on Main Street nearing Northern National Bank, the weary officer was surprised to find it empty and eerily quiet. Thinking it an odd contrast that virtually the whole town turned out for a fire but when the bank was robbed, no one seemed particularly interested. Arriving at the bank, he was amazed to find it closed and everyone gone, much as if to say another workday was over and it was time to go home.

Shortly after, a deluge of law enforcement officials began converging on the Town of Mars Hill. Members of the Sheriff's Department, including Deputy Edgar Wheeler, and state troopers gathered on Main Street, clustered around the bank at the corner of Market and Main. Some members of the Mars Hill Fire Department joined them. Meeting with Fitzherbert, they formulated a plan. Roadblocks would be set up north of Mars Hill on Route 1 in Westfield and another south of Mars Hill on Route 1 in Blaine. The County Sheriff's Department, state troopers, and the Presque Isle Police Department would staff the roadblocks. Two hours elapsed from the time of the robbery before the roadblocks were in place. The remaining officers, including Acting Chief Fitzherbert and Deputy Wheeler, would span out over the surrounding area in search of a strangely dressed man with unruly hair hauling two large bags filled with cash.

The school dance being held at the grade school on Fort Street was interrupted. Someone announced that the bank had been robbed. Stuart Craig and most of his classmates spilled out into the night and walked the short half mile to Main Street. They encountered a sight they had never experienced before—more than a dozen of police cars with flashing lights lined the entire street.

Believing the owner of the gray Oldsmobile that had sped off when he'd arrived at the bank was one of the Mahaney brothers, Fitzherbert labored much of the night conducting a careful, thorough search east of town toward Mars Hill

Mountain where one of the brothers had a cabin. With his spotlight combing the fields along the Boynton and East Blaine Roads, he worked his way to the Mahaney cabin that was located on the East Blaine Road near the south end of the mountain. Finding it empty, he climbed onto the roof to see if the chimney was warm; it wasn't. Returning to town, he again searched the area around the potato storage houses behind the bank and along adjacent Mill Street next to Prestile Stream. He found no evidence of the bank robber.

Meanwhile, Deputy Sheriff Edgar Wheeler was also searching the fields between Prestile Stream and Mars Hill Mountain in his cruiser. At one point, he thought he saw movement in a potato field off the East Blaine Road. Stopping, he slowly surveyed the area with his search light but saw nothing except snow and empty frozen field. Wheeler also experienced a long, futile night.

Mars Hill high school junior varsity basketball coach Brian Blanchard had left practice at 7:00 p.m. that evening and traveled to Presque Isle with friends. Returning home, they were stopped at a roadblock in Westfield. Someone in the car jokingly asked, "What happened, someone rob a bank?" The astonishing response was comically ironic, "Yeah, in Mars Hill."

All efforts to locate the robber or any evidence

of his escape that night failed. He had apparently vanished without a trace.

The FBI, headed by Chief Investigator Ray Ross and accompanied by four agents, arrived the next morning to assume charge of the investigation. Taking up residence and establishing command headquarters in the Mid-Town Motel owned by Mark Carney's father, their immediate goals were threefold: definitively identify the robber, determine how he had escaped, and whether or not there were accomplices. Inexplicably, they never interviewed Acting Chief Fay Fitzherbert, the first law enforcement officer on the scene.

Based on Ola Orser's observations, Bernard should have been an early suspect but the FBI had not yet reached that conclusion. Conflicting testimony by witnesses and skepticism about the teller's veracity were at least part of the reason. State police issued bulletins describing the robber to be five feet three inches tall, weighing one hundred and forty pounds, and in his early twenties with shoulder length black hair; a near perfect depiction of Bernard, except for hair color.

How the robber had managed his getaway was a baffling mystery. The last person to see him was a hunter parked across the street when he departed the bank and disappeared into the dark. Initial speculation was that he had fled in the normal fashion, by vehicle. However, a more bizarre alternative was also being considered.

On the previous Halloween Eve, an Arabian horse had disappeared from a Mars Hill farm. A five-year-old gelding named Blaze belonging to Mrs. Stuart Smith had vanished and was believed stolen. Ella Bartley thought she'd heard the "clompety clomp" of hoof beats at about the time the robber departed. One theory: a modern-day version of Butch Cassidy had ridden off into the night on Smith's Arabian gelding Blaze.

An occasional equestrian, Bernard enjoyed horseback riding. When he lived with his Uncle Grover next door to Edgar and Dottie Wheeler in Bridgewater, he often rode their horses. There was at least a modicum of credibility to the comic speculation that the bank robber had affected a cowboy westernstyle escape.

On Saturday morning, several of Bernard's friends met at Al's Diner for coffee. The bank robbery was the only topic of conversation. Almost all of them guessed Bernard had committed the crime. One person wrote his name on a piece of paper and stored it away in his safe deposit box so he could later prove he'd made the correct prediction. The FBI may have been uncertain about the identity of the perpetrator, but there was little confusion at Al's Diner.

Led by the FBI, a massive search involving state police, Aroostook County Sheriff's Department, Border Patrol agents, U.S. Customs Service, Immigration and Naturalization Service, and the Royal Canadian Mounted Police in New Brunswick, Canada, continued throughout the day. No solid leads surfaced and the bank robber was presumed to have left the area. The roadblocks were lifted Saturday night. Prospects for quick resolution to the case appeared dim.

The Presque Isle *Star Herald* was more optimistic. Their reporter, V. Paul Reynolds wrote, "The odds are quite high that the Mars Hill robber will exchange his instant wealth for some long years in prison. As for the $110,248.96 that he quickly withdrew from the Mars Hill bank, well he probably won't even\ get a chance to spend it—at least not all of it."

Maine Bonding and Casualty insurance company offered a $2,500 reward for information leading to an arrest and conviction of the person who robbed the bank. The bank's insurer, they would have to reimburse Northern National Bank if the stolen money wasn't recovered.

Despite the extensive manhunt, no one had considered or searched nearby Prestile Stream.

• 5 •

The Escape

"Bernard was remarkable operating at night. In Vietnam, others would follow him after he'd been out at night and invariably find dead VC with their ears cut off. He never walked on trails, there was nothing like him at night."

—A friend

No one knew the area behind Northern National Bank better than Bernard. He and his childhood buddies had grown up exploring the long row of potato storage houses aligned next to the railroad tracks behind Main Street. More recently, he had worked in the potato house assembly lines. As a kid, he had spent countless days playing on the steep embankment along the shore of Prestile Stream just beyond the storage buildings on the opposite side of Mill Street. Every subtle detail was an indelible part of his consciousness; darkness was just a small obstacle. Which alleys were open between the potato houses, when he would cross the railroad tracks, and how far it was to the precipitous incline above the stream were all graphically etched in his mind. His late evening visit on the previous Friday had been his final rehearsal.

Operating in darkness was a very unique asset for Bernard. To survive as a tunnel rat, he had perfected the art of visually adapting to the dark. Moving with stealth in a nocturnal world while performing intricate tasks had become instinctive for him. The many nights in Vietnamese jungles seeking out the enemy had further enhanced his exceptional skill. Navigating through the alleys between the potato houses at night was an exercise he had unwittingly practiced innumerable times before. Counting the steps to the railroad tracks and negotiating the steep descent to Prestile Stream without being detected was a no brainer, even with the strenuous burden of hauling two unwieldy bags of money.

Except during periods of high water, the level on Prestile Stream is controlled by a dam just above Fort Street on the north end of town. The water level was normal that night. A shallow, quick flowing brook, it meanders somewhat circuitously in a southerly direction generally parallel to Mill Street. Typical of New England mill streams at the time, it was badly polluted. Potato waste, discharge from a starch factory, and other effluence spilled unimpeded into the water. The town dump, situated on the west bank just off Mill Street, contributed additional contaminants. Given its toxic condition, Prestile Stream was rarely used for recreational purposes. With the exception of Bernard, no one considered it to be a viable avenue for travel.

Departing Mars Hill, Prestile Stream drifts swiftly through the Town of Blaine, past the tiny village of Robinsons and crosses the Canadian border into the Province of New Brunswick after seven miles. In New Brunswick, it assumes its Franco-moniker, Presquile Stream. Flowing for a few more miles, Presquile Stream joins the St. John River, the most substantial river in the Maritime Provinces. Confident that law enforcement officials would not anticipate his downriver escape, that was Bernard's destination. Self-sufficiency, safety, and financial independence were just a few hours of paddling downstream to Canada.

Having wrestled his awkward bundles of money down the precipitous, densely wooded embankment, Bernard reached his getaway vehicle carefully parked on the shore of Prestile Stream, a bright orange inflatable kayak. In theory, the lightweight watercraft was an excellent choice for this shallow body of water. Given its buoyancy, the inflatable boat displaced very little water allowing paddler and boat to ride high clearing the gravely, often rock-strewn streambed that was concealed just below the surface in many places. However, the flimsy kayak with a high center of gravity was not designed to carry heavy loads.

Casting aside his wig and trench coat, Bernard loaded the two large bundles of money into the kayak that was already laden with camping gear and food supplies. Grabbing his paddle and throwing himself on top, he unsteadily launched his boat into the fast moving current. His journey to freedom and a new life had begun. Carrying over 250 pounds of unbalanced weight was too much of a burden for the tiny, unstable craft. Immediately capsizing, he and all contents were unceremoniously spilled into the frigid quick water.

The icy, fast moving water had a stultifying, penetrating impact, leaving him stunned, flailing, and breathless. Gasping for air, Bernard staggered to gain his balance and stand upright against the strong current. Up to his waist in potato sewage and forty degree water, he desperately struggled to regain his composure. Frantically swimming and thrashing about with minimal visibility, he retrieved most of the gear, supplies, and the two bags of money. Righting and carefully reloading the kayak, he again continued his downstream voyage. The weight of the waterlogged gear and bags of money was simply too much, the boat swamped and ran aground.

After two attempts, Bernard had traveled a

mere fifty yards in his unusual getaway vessel. Most of his gear was soaked and he had two bags containing over $110,000 of soggy cash in small denominations, including 20,000 one dollar bills. His clothing was beginning to freeze and he started to sneeze and shiver violently. Hypothermia and desperation were beginning to overwhelm him.

Lights came on in a nearby house. Fearing that his noisy sufferings had alerted the inhabitants, Bernard silently concealed the useless vessel under some brush at the bottom of the riverbank along the east shore of the stream. Barely able to feel his legs and frozen hands, he carelessly shoved wet gear and supplies into his backpack. Lifting the heavy pack onto his back, he numbly staggered out across a snow covered field dragging two bags of money that now weighed almost one hundred pounds.

Although laboring mightily, his heavy load had one distinct advantage. The exertion expended carrying the weighty, cumbersome burden while wading in several inches of snow warmed his core body temperature and feeling began to return to his hands, legs, and feet. Wandering easterly toward Mars Hill Mountain, he decided to seek temporary refuge in a cabin belonging to a family member. Arriving there, no one was home. Concerned that his family might be implicated in the robbery, he hurriedly exchanged his wet clothes and camping gear for dry replacements and quickly departed. Shortly after leaving, he observed a police cruiser speeding in his direction with siren blaring and blue lights flashing. His combat experience instinctively kicked in, he immediately hit the ground face first, burrowing deeply into the snow.

As the cruiser proceeded past, he recognized that it was Deputy Sheriff Edgar Wheeler's vehicle. Bernard knew Deputy Wheeler well and liked him. A neighbor of his uncle Grover, it was Wheeler who had recently confiscated his driver's license for reckless driving. Realizing his vulnerability in an open field, he began working away from the road toward a stand of trees. Wheeler returned, this time driving much slower as he passed. Again Bernard dove into the snow as Wheeler moved along at an agonizingly plodding speed. Reminded of many much warmer yet similarly traumatic encounters in Vietnam, Bernard, his face ignominiously buried in the wet, freezing snow, instinctively realized that he must remain completely stationary while lying prostrate on this frigid carpet of snow until the enemy had vanished into the night.

Again Bernard stumbled toward the shelter of trees dragging his hefty load in several inches of snow. Wheeler returned for a third time. Changing his pattern, he stopped and scrutinized the area surveying the field several times with his spotlight. Rushing for cover, Bernard fell on something large, furry, and vile smelling just as the beam of light passed over his diving body. Whatever it was didn't move and neither did he. After illuminating the field for several more minutes, Wheeler relented and left. Carefully rising, he kicked the object. Completely lifeless, it was a dead bear.

Cold, weary, and his plan in disarray, Bernard still had reason for optimism. He'd experienced many much worse nights in Vietnam and always survived. He was confident he would again.

Now without a coherent scheme, he pushed on until completely exhausted. Finding a small, narrow ditch that provided some limited shelter, he crawled into his sleeping bag after donning all of the dry clothes he was carrying to help insulate him from the cold. Snow flurries were falling when he collapsed asleep. Twelve hours later, Bernard awoke covered in a light layer of snow to find he was quite visible from the road, and his very obvious resting place provided an excellent view of the town of Mars Hill below. This kind of mental error would have proved fatal in the world he'd recently left, he thought. He'd be dead or a prisoner of war in Vietnam.

Unlike Vietnam where he was almost always

70

unfamiliar with the terrain, few people knew the Mars Hill Mountain area better than Bernard. He had family and friends who owned or squatted on property on the backside of the mountain. Using their cabins as a base, he had explored the entire mountain during his youth. After returning from Vietnam, he had often taken dates on motorcycle rides on the roads around the mountain because there was little chance of his being seen and arrested for driving without a license. On one occasion, he had attempted to climb the Mars Hill Ski Area service road on his bike. Despite a valiant effort, he didn't make the summit.

Urgently needing to find concealment before he was spotted, crawling and crouching he dragged his gear to the comparative security of a nearby wooded area. Pondering his fate while eating a can of cold beans, he remembered a secluded location deep in the woods on the backside of Mars Hill Mountain where he'd camped as a kid. Bernard spent the day bushwhacking and thrashing through thick underbrush for over a mile until reaching his old campsite. Situated next to an overhanging ledge about head high, surrounded by fir trees, he was able to erect a crude shelter with a small tarp in much the same fashion he'd used his army half tent in the military.

Soon after, it was dark. Lying in his sleeping

bag, he contemplated his circumstance. Less than twenty-four hours had elapsed since he'd relieved Northern National Bank of most of its money. It seemed like a month had transpired. He had more money than he'd ever dreamed but no way to spend it. Instead, he was confined to the side of a mountain hiding under a lean-to with a few cans of beans and a canteen of water. The temperature was below freezing but he didn't dare start a fire. The only value the money had provided so far was damp insulation. Tomorrow he would think of something, he concluded as he drifted off to sleep.

Bernard would remain in his hideout for several days. Eating a can of cold beans daily, he filled his canteen with snow every night melting it in the sleeping bag next to his body while he slept. He was the beneficiary of an exceptional stretch of good weather, especially for northern Maine in mid-November. Temperatures were cold but tolerable. For the first three days, highs were in the thirties and twenties at night time. On Tuesday, there was a warm-up into the thirties and forties that lasted for another three days. After the snow flurries on the night of the robbery, there was no precipitation through Thursday.

On the seventh night, he was frightened awake by something heavy sitting on top of him. His first thought was that Deputy Wheeler was standing over him with one boot on his chest. He screamed in terror. The petrified animal, whatever it was, dashed into the woods. Badly shaken and out of food, Bernard knew that he had to move on.

Freezing rain was pelting the tarp when he awoke on Friday morning. A cold, raw miserable morning, at least the stormy weather would provide cover and a distraction making him less likely to be identified when he returned to civilization. After stuffing about $17,000 into a coffee can and burying it next to the road leading to Mars Hill Mountain, Bernard shoved the remaining damp, partially frozen money into his backpack, walked out of the woods, and hiked down the Boynton Road into the Town of Mars Hill.

Defiantly unafraid, he ambled south on Main Street in the rain past Al's Diner opposite FBI temporary headquarters in the Mid-Town Motel and by the bank he'd robbed a week earlier now carrying more than $93,000 of its money in his pack. No one paid any attention as he stepped into the phone booth next to the Rexall Drug Store and called his cousin David Patterson in Presque Isle.

A short time later, David, who would be convicted of murdering his wife a couple of years later, picked him up at a potato house at the end of Market Street and drove him to his place in Presque Isle. He remained in the Presque Isle area recuperating and visiting with friends for two days. Spending some of his time at the University of Maine in Presque Isle, he ate, socialized, and rested. While there, he learned that law enforcement officials had been inquiring about him. Any thoughts of remaining in the area eliminated, Bernard had to find a way to leave northern Maine.

While buying pot during his second night in Presque Isle, he met two Canadian drug dealers who agreed to drive him to Connecticut for $500. The next day the three of them drove south through Mars Hill sharing a joint as they passed Northern National Bank where Bernard had made off with the largest bank haul in the history of the State of Maine. Just beyond, they passed directly by Deputy Wheeler on his way to lunch at Smith's Truck Stop. Sitting in the back seat partially stoned, Bernard thought they'd made eye contact.

Born the son of a poor local family turned war hero, now wealthy Bernard Patterson was leaving Mars Hill in the foggy haze of marijuana smoke—rich and free.

• 6 •

The Investigation

". . . he had a hard life, never knew
him to be in trouble before."
—Mars Hill resident

While Bernard was concealed under a flimsy, weathered tarp on Mars Hill Mountain a mere three and a half miles away, the largest law enforcement investigation in the history of northern Maine was under way in the Town of Mars Hill. Consisting of the FBI, state, county, and local police; Border Patrol, U.S. Customs Service, and the Royal Canadian Mounted Police were also on high-priority alert. For about two weeks, the correlation of law enforcement officers to the population in Mars Hill almost exceeded their average teacher-to-student classroom ratio. The community was inundated with investigators interrogating the citizenry. No one in Mars Hill had ever experienced anything remotely like it.

The FBI didn't arrive in Mars Hill until the Saturday morning after the robbery. Directed by senior agent Ray Ross, the FBI assumed control of the investigation because bank robbery is a federal crime. Ross had the reputation of being a thorough no-nonsense investigator, not prone to conjecture or guess work. The initial theory was that the unidentified robber had escaped in a getaway vehicle although there were no witnesses after he had left the bank. The predominant assumption was that the masked bandit had fled the area prior to establishment of the roadblocks, perhaps entering New Brunswick, Canada, just a few miles away.

Acting Police Chief Fay Fitzherbert was the initial law enforcement officer on the scene and the first official to interrogate bank employees and witnesses to the robbery. Mystifyingly, he was never formally interviewed by the FBI. Those primarily responsible for conducting the investigation did not have the immediate knowledge that Fitzherbert possessed. They didn't know that he had witnessed a gray Oldsmobile leaving the scene when he arrived at the bank and that Ola Orser had informed him minutes after the robbery had taken place that she recognized the robber as Bernard Patterson. Both Fitzherbert and Deputy Sheriff Wheeler had scoured the lower mountain area east of town by vehicle after the robbery and would continue to do so in the days following. However, no thorough, significant off-road search effort was ever commenced on Mars Hill Mountain.

Internal bank auditors arrived at Northern National Bank and a comprehensive audit was conducted to determine how much money had been stolen and whether or not there was an indication of possible employee involvement. Each teller was exhaustively interviewed and a meticulous accounting of records at their individual work stations was completed. As proof machine operator, teller Martha Lawrence determined what the beginning balances had been, what transactions had occurred during the day, and what the ending balance should be. Exactly $110,214.96 was missing. Using the Consumer Price Index as a guide, the current value of that amount would be about $700,000. Auditors found no evidence of employee complicity.

An early focus of the investigation was an attempt to determine who had made the phone call reporting the fire just prior to the robbery. A woman had called in the alarm to the Aroostook Health Center a few minutes before eight. Since the Mars Hill Fire Department was a volunteer force, if there was no answer at the fire station or the chief's residence, the calls rang on a fire line at the nearby hospital that was staffed twenty-four hours a day. Two phone calls had been received.

The first phone call was answered by nurse Elva Garrison. The caller had a young woman's voice and Garrison also heard a man and woman talking in the background. She couldn't quite understand them and thought they were whispering. Apparently confused when Garrison answered on behalf of the health center, the caller hung up. Calling a second time, a young woman told nurse Alice Morse that there was a fire on A.C.I. Street and again hung up without providing any additional explanation. Morse turned in the alarm. The almost universal presumption was that the woman caller was an accomplice. Early efforts to identify that caller were unsuccessful.

The fire that had occurred on Clark Road the Friday before the robbery was also a focal point of the investigation. Both the property owner, Duane Grass, and many other local fire and law enforcement officials believed it was arson and the evidence generally supported that conclusion. Investigators saw two potential relationships with the robbery. One possibility was that the fire was set with the intent of robbing the bank that night but something had gone awry. Another was that starting the fire had been an experiment to see how local officials would react. If that was the intent, it had been an instructive success as all of the town law enforcement and fire officials along with a significant portion of the citizens had turned out. Either way, a connection between the fire and the robbery appeared probable. Evidence associating anyone with the fire was nonexistent and there had been several unsolved arsons in the area in recent months.

The exceptionally large amount of money in the bank at the time of the robbery was also a matter of scrutiny. Whether or not the robber had inside knowledge or assistance were considerations. Had someone tipped him off about the large Brink's cash delivery earlier that day? The bank vault was not always open, why was it unlocked on the night of the robbery? Or was the robber the beneficiary of an extraordinary amount of good fortune?

Bank employees were possible suspects. While this consideration was an inherent part of standard investigatory procedures, that line of examination distracted from other very relevant factors. Ola Orser's belief that Bernard was the robber was not given serious credence during the early phase of the inquiry. The fact that the tellers knew he'd been a frequent visitor at the bank in the weeks leading up to the crime was not initially discussed with the FBI. When that information finally surfaced, law enforcement officials wondered why such suspicious behavior hadn't been reported to authorities prior to the robbery.

Since the Arabian horse Blaze had been missing for nearly two weeks and presumed stolen, cursory speculation was given to the possibility that the robber had escaped on horseback. The only other evidence supporting this supposition was witness Ella Bartley's observation that she'd heard hoof beats right after the robbery. No one had reported seeing a white stallion galloping through town that night carrying a clownishly dressed rider and two large bags, a singularly unusual sight that would have instantly captured the attention of even the most bored onlooker. Ironically, Bernard had occasionally enjoyed riding Deputy Sheriff Edgar Wheeler's horses when he had stayed with his uncle Grover who lived next door to Wheeler and his wife Dottie. A getaway vehicle continued to be the assumed method of escape.

Two days after the robbery, Acting Chief Fitzherbert stopped what he believed was the same gray Oldsmobile that had sped off when he had arrived at the bank on the night of the robbery. Gary Mahaney was the driver and Fitzherbert found him to be evasive. Since the stop was based on an inspection violation, there was no probable cause to detain him or search the car, so he was released.

Smoke was reported on a ledge behind a cabin on the back side of Mars Hill Mountain on the Tuesday following the robbery. Located just a short distance from the Canadian border, a team of investigators rushed to the scene including Acting Chief Fitzherbert and several FBI agents. Fitzherbert searched the area behind the cabin and found nothing suspicious and no indication of a fire. The FBI agents never left their vehicle. Bernard was huddled in his wilderness hideout less than a half mile away. Even after this episode, no thorough search of Mars Hill Mountain was initiated.

As the investigation progressed, evidence implicating Bernard as the robber accumulated. He had been missing since the time of the robbery. Most of the witnesses agreed on a description that fit him; although complicating the issue somewhat one customer had a different recollection of the robber's size, thinking him a large man. Ola Orser's assertion that she had recognized him at the time of the robbery was finally considered credible. And no one else had been identified as the likely bandit. By Thursday, Bernard was deemed the primary suspect. A cloak of secrecy was maintained surrounding the entire investigation and this revelation was not released to the public.

On Friday morning November 19, Bernard walked into town. Disheveled and carrying a large pack stuffed with damp, icy money, he nonchalantly strode down Main Street in the rain passing within one hundred feet of FBI headquarters at the Mid-Town Motel. While investigators continued to comb the area questioning people, he proceeded through town unnoticed and unmolested. Other than law enforcement officials, no one knew Bernard was definitely a suspect; although several of his friends presumed he was the robber. The following Monday, he traveled through town a second time on his way to Connecticut. Again, Bernard went undetected in the midst of a massive manhunt for him.

Once the investigation was concentrated on Bernard, detectives gave additional consideration to who had placed the false fire alarm call. Bernard's girlfriend or girlfriends were people of interest. He was believed to have lived with a woman in Bangor for a short time prior to the robbery and had several romantic interests in the Mars Hill area. No evidence was found linking any of his female friends with the phone call or robbery.

After two weeks, the investigation was at a dead end. Authorities could find no one who admitted to having seen Bernard since the night of the robbery. They had no leads on his method of escape or where he might have gone. No evidence existed associating anyone else with the crime. Completely baffled, the FBI left town.

On December 3, 1971, three weeks after the

robbery, the U.S. Attorney's office in Bangor issued a warrant for Bernard's arrest for the November 12 holdup of Northern National Bank. He was the only person charged. Ray Ross and his team of FBI agents were credited with a successful investigation that led to his being identified as the sole robber and charged with the crime. The next day, Deputy Sheriff Wheeler announced that the November sitting of the State of Maine Grand Jury had indicted Bernard for the August 14 burglary of Al's Diner based on an investigation completed by Deputy Sheriff Luke Weider. Bernard's friend David Bradbury had previously been arrested for the crime.

Many Mars Hill residents were surprised and saddened with the announcement that a well-known local boy had been identified as a burglar and bank robber. Reminiscing about a young man who had grown up in the community, attended local schools, went off to war and returned a hero, they struggled to explain his behavior. One person remembered him as an "untroublesome lad though he had a hard life, never knew him to be in trouble before." Another woman added, "He was alright until he came home from the army." An acquaintance recalled a conversation with him in which he'd stated he knew he had to finish high school and go to college if he was to "make anything of himself." Despite his misdeeds, he was still almost universally liked and few people were inclined to criticize him.

A Federal Grand Jury hearing was held on Monday, January 17, 1972, in Bangor Federal Court regarding the Mars Hill robbery. Among those subpoenaed were witnesses Ola Orser and Ella Bartley and law enforcement officers Edgar Wheeler and Luke Weider. The Presque Isle *Star Herald* reported that although all Grand Jury proceedings are secret, an exceptionally high level of secrecy surrounded this inquiry as government officials, including U.S. Attorney Peter Mills, would not even acknowledge that a hearing was being held or that an indictment was being sought against Bernard Patterson.

Since a warrant for Bernard's arrest had already been issued, speculation about the purpose of a Grand Jury hearing was rampant. Prevailing law enforcement theory was that Bernard had escaped to Canada. A Grand Jury indictment would provide legal justification for Canadian officials to issue a warrant for his arrest and facilitate extradition. Another possibility was that accomplices had been identified and were being considered. Bernard was the only person indicted.

A legal strategy for extradition from a foreign country was a logical plan, but Canada was the wrong choice. By the time of the Grand Jury hearing, Bernard was on a different continent, 3,500 miles away living the high life.

• 7 •

Trans America

"Bernard was not a bad person. They put him in a shit hole and he came out tougher and stronger. He was just a country boy who got drafted."
—Doug Pierce, a friend

Leaving Mars Hill late morning, driving was slow and hazardous on the first day of their trip to Connecticut. Traveling through dense fog and rain on slippery roads in a ten-year-old Volkswagen Bus, Bernard and his two pot-smoking French Canadian companions were only able to average about fifty miles per hour for most of the day. Considering their lack of sobriety, that speed was excessive.

Pierre and Richard were unaware of the robbery or the contents of Bernard's pack and he had no intention of disclosing it. His newly formulated plan was to locate Vietnam army buddies on the West Coast and was not inclined to share his recently acquired windfall with people he hardly knew. Since the Canadians were functioning in a very marginal state of consciousness, he had little to be concerned about. Carrying several pounds of marijuana to sell at colleges in the Boston and Hartford areas, they perceived Bernard to be just another spaced-out hippy pothead. Living at the pinnacle of the Woodstock generation era, their world was replete with drugged-up peaceniks in search of something to protest while existing from one high to the next. That this flower child was in truth a certified warrior just a few months removed from combat would have been a completely unsuspected revelation. Although all three had excellent reasons to cautiously avoid encounters with law enforcement, that wasn't apparent as they were oblivious to the numerous police cars they passed while drinking beer and regularly sharing joints journeying south in the inclement weather.

When heavy freezing rain developed as temperatures dropped after dark, driving became impossible and the imprudent trio was forced to stop at a small motel in Portsmouth, New Hampshire. Ravenous after a day of smoking pot, drinking beer, and nothing to eat except a bag of chips, Bernard sprung for food and drink at a nearby pub. Steaks, seafood, and the very best wines were their dining selections. He was living the high life now and thoroughly enjoying it. The waitress was ecstatic when she received a $50 tip.

Weather improved the following day for their remaining drive to Windsor Locks, Connecticut. Located a few miles east of Bradley Field, the largest airport in the Hartford area, Bernard had his almost perpetually stoned Canadian escorts deliver him to the recently built resort, Hills Point Hotel. These were the most upscale accommodations he could locate after a brief survey of the community. Still high, Pierre and Richard sold him an ounce of pot and departed in search of lucrative sales opportunities at the nearby Springfield College campus.

They drove south to the outskirts of Hartford before the foolhardy pair realized they had been traveling in the wrong direction for about fifteen miles; it was the following day before they finally arrived at the college. Without Bernard to do the navigating, the remainder of their trip would be a delusional, circuitous, yet profitable pilgrimage. Amazingly, despite their chaotic, irrational behavior, they were never apprehended and safely returned to Canada flush with American cash after liquidating their hallucinogenic inventory.

After checking into the resort, Bernard hired a cab to transport him to town where he visited a barber for a shave and much needed haircut. Later, the cabbie chauffeured him to local stores where he bought a new suit of clothes: a London Fog coat and a pair of Joe Willie Namath boots.

Appearing and feeling dapper after returning and showering at the hotel, he spent the evening buying drinks at the bar while regaling customers and an attractive blonde bartender with salacious, disarming tales about night life in Saigon. Happiest when he had money, Bernard was quickly developing an affinity for his recently acquired wealth. Quite enamored with the bartender, she was another blissful recipient of Bernard's largesse.

Well groomed and sporting his new attire while still carrying a battered, grievously weathered pack loaded with damp cash and an ounce of pot, Bernard was a study in contrasts when he entered Murphy Terminal at Bradley Field International Airport on the morning of Thanksgiving Eve, November 24. Unable to find a direct flight to California, he settled for a connector route through Houston, Texas, to Los Angeles. Steadfastly refusing to be separated from his cash, he shouldered his cumbersome, offensive pack as a carry-on. Self-assuredly acknowledging numerous curious, incredulous stares from passengers and flight attendants, he belatedly realized his incongruent pack made him extremely conspicuous. Upgrading his luggage was an obvious requirement if he was to do any additional traveling.

While in flight to California, another remarkable crime was perhaps coincidentally playing out in the skies over the northwestern United States. At 2:50 p.m., PST, Northwest Orient Flight 305 departed from Portland, Oregon for Seattle, Washington. A passenger later known as D. B. Cooper threatened to blow up the Boeing 727 unless $200,000 in cash and four parachutes were delivered to him after landing at Seattle-Tacoma Airport. When the ransom was dispatched as instructed, the commercial jet and a skeleton crew departed Seattle at 7:40 p.m. for his stipulated destination of Mexico City via Reno, Nevada. Less than thirty-five minutes later, at 8:13 p.m., Cooper opened the rear exit door from the unpressurized cabin, deployed the aft staircase and parachuted into the night somewhere over Washington State carrying 10,000 unmarked twenty dollar bills. Presumed to have landed in an area south of Mount St. Helens, despite an intensive, massive manhunt, he was never found. Having enjoyed several drinks and leaving a very liberal gratuity with a comely dark-haired stewardess while en route, Bernard arrived in Los Angeles a short time after Cooper's astonishing midflight departure.

Although no evidence has ever surfaced to link Cooper and Bernard, their apparent personality similarities and the timing of their dramatic crimes and escapes are extraordinary. An alias, D. B. Cooper's true identity has never been determined. Exhibiting a calm, fearless demeanor throughout the skyjacking, perhaps he was a former tunnel rat. Possibly he and Bernard were friends or had endured subterranean combat together in Vietnam. Could he have been a disenchanted war veteran or suffering from posttraumatic stress disorder? The answer seems to be, quite possibly.

The FBI didn't believe that Cooper could have survived the jump but they couldn't find Bernard in the tiny town of Mars Hill either. The danger of plummeting out of the Boeing 727, which had been slowed to about 120 miles per hour and was flying at 10,000 feet, would have compared in risk with some of the harrowing episodes encountered in the tunnels of Cu Chi. Many skydiving experts believe that someone with sufficient military experience could have successfully completed the jump and subsequently survived if adequate provisions and equipment had been properly secreted away in advance. A common thread in all of their assumptions was the need for significant military training and experience. Bernard certainly had it and conceivably D. B. Cooper possessed it too.

Four months later, on April 7, 1972, Richard Floyd McCoy, Jr., another heavily decorated Vietnam War veteran, hijacked United Airlines Flight 855 bound from Denver, Colorado. Armed with a toy hand grenade and an empty pistol, he secured a $500,000 ransom. A D. B. Cooper copycat, he also made a midflight parachute jump and safely landed. Unlike Bernard and Cooper, McCoy was quickly apprehended having only spent $30.

Once settled in a hotel at Los Angeles International Airport, Bernard began attempting to contact his former army buddies. Fellow tunnel rat Corporal Emilio Gonzales had reenlisted and was believed to be back in Vietnam. Another reenlistee was 101st Airborne Division tracker, Tom "T Man" Maury. Several others had simply disappeared—perhaps one of them had recently parachuted into the darkness from Northwest Orient Flight 305. Initially, he was unable to find any information on former platoon leader and close friend Bruce Hakala. Bernard was despondent; he had a small fortune to spend and no one to share the fast life with him.

Finally, after several hours of phone calls and searching directories, he located Bruce, who was unexpectedly attending law school at UCLA. Meeting at a motel near the university, Bernard informed him that he had accumulated a large sum of cash in the black market while serving in Vietnam, stating that he was on the run as he was being investigated by both military and civilian law enforcement authorities. Neither revelation was a surprising disclosure to Bruce. Intending to ensure that Bruce would not be implicated in the bank robbery, Bernard scrupulously avoided informing him of the true source of the money. Considering various options, they decided on a skiing vacation in Switzerland as soon as the UCLA fall semester ended on December 3.

A college dropout from the University of Minnesota, Bruce had grown up on a dairy farm a few miles north of Minneapolis-St. Paul. An antiwar activist, he was drafted into the army in July 1966. After boot camp, he was selected for Officer Candidate School (OCS) at Fort Benning, Georgia. Believing that being an officer would improve the quality of his time in the service, he accepted the OCS training appointment. Sent directly to Vietnam after graduating, Second Lieutenant Hakala was assigned to the 25th Infantry Division as a platoon leader in the Cu Chi sector in February 1967. The platoon's noncommissioned officer was Sergeant Bernard Patterson, who had been leading the platoon for a month after the previous platoon leader had died instantly after he was shot through the head by friendly fire during tunnel operations. The previous platoon leader had just lowered himself into a narrow tunnel entrance to communicate with Bernard and had violated the cardinal tunnel rat rule to always whistle Dixie when popping back out of a hole. A jittery platoon member had shot first and asked questions after. He was the third platoon leader Bernard had lost as a result of combat death.

A peace loving, antiwar protester turned soldier, Bruce had no intention of following in his predecessor's footsteps. He had a singular driving obsession, finish his one-year tour of duty and return home safely. Since avoiding dangerous situations was paramount in his mind, he would try to get assigned to the relative safety of the rear echelon as quickly as possible. In the interim, entering the tunnels was purely voluntary. He would lead the platoon from above the ground. That was fine with Bernard, who had wearied of young, inexperienced second lieutenants who were so adept at getting themselves and others in the platoon killed or injured. He preferred to be in charge.

Bruce's commitment to peace and self-preservation ended when Bernard dragged one of his "rats," a twenty-year-old Puerto Rican corporal, out of a hole. A bamboo lance had been shoved through his throat when he'd opened a trap door and peered above. He slowly died desperately gasping for air and gagging up blood while Bernard, Bruce, and others in the platoon waited in vain for requested medical assistance. Enraged, Bruce now had a more compelling motive: revenge.

Imposing on Bernard to educate him in the

rules of the underground world of tunnels, Bruce was now committed to not just his own safety but the protection of all of his "rats." And he fully intended to exact a terrible toll on an enemy he now hated with a greater passion than any he had ever known. He quickly learned that there was no rank in the tunnels. The leader was the shrewdest, wiliest, calmest most aggressive of all. Bernard was the leader. Almost six feet tall and a little heavy, Bruce was by most standards too big to be a "rat." But he had an outstanding mentor and learned well. He rapidly acquired a mental and physical toughness he never knew he possessed. He learned never to fire more than three shots from his revolver without reloading because the enemy would know when he was out of ammo, how to set demolition charges to maximize entombing the enemy, recognizing the signs of booby traps and how and when to open a trap door. Bernard taught him to listen for and smell the enemy. And he always loudly whistled Dixie when he crawled out of a hole. One trait could not be taught; he never acquired Bernard's fearlessness. Bruce was normal; he wanted to go home alive and uninjured.

The respect between Bernard and Bruce was substantial and palpable. They functioned as a well lubricated team—brothers in combat. At a time when fragging was quite common, covertly executing unpopular or incompetent officers, Bernard always had Bruce's back. One of the few officers who regularly went down into the tunnels, Bernard had tremendous admiration for him. During the remainder of his tour, Bruce never lost another "rat" in his platoon.

After completing his one-year tour of duty, Bruce returned home with a Bronze Star for valor and a Purple Heart for a relatively minor grenade injury. He declined to extend his tour of duty, left the service and went back to college. After obtaining his undergraduate degree with high honors at San Diego State College, he was accepted at UCLA Law School where he simultaneously immersed himself in the antiwar movement that was flourishing in Southern California. Bernard's unexpected arrival was bittersweet. The mutual respect and friendship was still there, but Bruce was trying to mentally leave Vietnam behind and had acquired a newfound goal in life. Cesar Chavez had inspired him to advocate for migrant workers after he graduated from law school. A potato picker in his youth, Bernard related to the migrant workers.

Bernard had come to the realization that traveling for him was now potentially hazardous, especially airline travel to a foreign country. Although uncertain, he had to assume that by now law enforcement authorities had identified him as the bank robber and bulletins with his picture were being circulated. In fact, the FBI had still not made a determination that he was the primary suspect and no public announcement had been made.

Cooper's skyjacking had further complicated airline travel for everyone as the crime had created an immense amount of interest world-wide and a profound focus on air safety. Television media and newspapers were consumed with articles and speculation about the sensational crime. Safety and prevention of further skyjackings now an elevated priority, heightened airline security and scrutiny would be a virtual certainty at terminals everywhere and especially during international flights. Despite added awareness and precautions, an abundance of copycat skyjackings quickly followed.

If Bernard was going to be a world traveler and bon vivant while avoiding capture, he needed a new identity.

• 8 •

Transformation

"(In Vietnam) he got used to having lots of money and a lawless environment where he made the rules."
—Mark Carney, friend

Two very significant obstacles confronted Bernard if he was to assume the role of a sophisticated, high-rolling international globe-trotter. He needed to obtain a passport with a new identity and find a way to inconspicuously transport more than $90,000 dollars in cash through foreign customs.

Purchase of traditional tourist airline luggage would be at least a partial solution to smuggling the money. A healthy infusion of good luck would also be a necessity. However, acquiring a new identity and a passport with his photo was essential and a predicament that did not lend itself to an obvious, simple solution.

Contemplating these dilemmas did not stop Bernard from immediately becoming a very active participant in the local party scene. With

Bruce's connections, an abundance of personal charm and possessing copious amounts of cash he was anxious to spend, he promptly immersed himself in the Southern California subculture of drugs, free love, and the avant-garde, psychedelic music scene. Although money was not an issue that now concerned him, free love was still particularly appealing to Bernard.

Since Bernard had spent most of the previous four years in the military in Vietnam and much of the rest of his life living in the comparatively sheltered environment of northern Maine, he had little first-hand experience with the revolutionary cultural changes that began taking place in much of the United States during the mid-1960s. California was at the epicenter of that movement. Antiwar sentiments or advocacy for radical political ideologies had little fascination for him.

While Bernard didn't necessarily share or fully understand the government's anti-communist, domino theory justification for the war, he accepted President Johnson's admonition that if the Communists weren't stopped in Vietnam they'd have to be halted in Hawaii or on the shores of California. He was generally supportive of the administration's Vietnamese policy based on a more limited view related to his own personal experiences. In his mind, the enemy represented evil and American soldiers should be supported. Bernard's political views were quite traditional, considering himself a capitalist who had simply collected overdue severance pay for services rendered. He very much appreciated the benefits of the free market system, particularly quality accommodations, good food, and drink. What did attract Bernard about the social upheaval he found in Southern California were the vast numbers of young, sexually liberated women and the availability of drugs, particularly marijuana. Pragmatically, he embraced those aspects of the revolution that tempted him or met his needs while ignoring the rest.

At his first party, he met an enchanting twenty-one-year-old flower child who had rejected her birth name and assumed the moniker Lunar Eclipse. Petite, pretty, charming, and completely uninhibited, he was instantaneously enamored. She found his harsh, unsympathetic view of the world coupled with good looks and a likeable personality the perfect challenge; an opportunity to use her sexual charms to convert him to her newfound philosophy of world peace, love, and harmony. While not necessarily an easy convert, Bernard was a willing participant in any experimentation she might devise to make his romantic world a better place.

Lunar personified many, perhaps most, of the so-called liberated young women living on the

UCLA campus at the time. Thoroughly indoctrinated by the counterculture movement as a teenager during the late 1960s, she embraced every aspect. She stopped wearing a bra, grew her hair down below her waist, and was committed to having sex with as many partners as possible, male or female. A dedicated reporter for the college underground newspaper, she regularly smoked pot, dabbled in hallucinogenic drugs, and almost perpetually listened to psychedelic music. An ardent supporter of the Black Panthers, Lunar idolized Che Guevara and thought she was a devoted Marxist without having a coherent understanding of its underlying principles. She simply knew that materialism was corrupt and immoral. That she was the beneficiary of a substantial trust fund resulting from the workings of the free market and regularly received considerable financial support from her capitalist parents did not impress her as contradictory.

Born Angela Liebowitz, Lunar was the only child of upper middle-class Jewish parents who owned several clothing stores in the Santa Barbara area. They sent her to private schools, exclusive summer camps, and otherwise materially doted on her. They did not receive the intended result as she was a naïve, gullible flower child who rejected virtually all of their traditional and religious values. She marched in protest against the war and various other causes, was jailed once for chaining herself to a fire truck during a feminist rally, believed capitalism was a vile, predatory economic system, and was firmly convinced that collectivism was the answer to all of society's economic and social problems. God was dead and spiritualism was best found in drugs, marriage was an anachronistic institution, and, most important to Bernard, sex should be openly shared with others in a communal environment. Bernard was an enthusiastic believer in free love.

Bernard and Lunar spent their first night together sharing a beach house owned by her parents with three of Lunar's other lovers: two UCLA coeds and a speed freak named Robert Peter Inman. Besides a wild night of sex and drugs, it was a fortuitous interlude for Bernard. Inman looked remarkably like him in both size and facial features and lacked a trust fund or wealthy, adoring parents.

Inman was not a student at UCLA or anywhere else. However, he had an unofficial degree in the science of human behavior. He specialized in living off other people, especially the ingenuous adherents to the counterculture who willingly supplied him with food, drugs, money, and sex. When he wore out his welcome or tired of one relationship, he found another innocent victim or victims. The supply seemed endless.

In perpetual need of money, Inman had obtained a passport to facilitate his occasional visits to Central America to purchase drugs for others or resale. Bernard had plenty of money and found that with a change in his haircut and a fake mustache, he was a virtual carbon copy of Inman's passport picture. Never thinking more than a brief moment into the future, Inman sold him the passport for $400. A luxurious European ski vacation now looked like a distinct possibility for the two former tunnel rats about to become cosmopolitan tourists. A remarkable coincidence was evolving 2,700 miles away. On June 1, 1971, the badly beaten, semi-nude sexually molested body of seventy-four-year-old Charlotte Dunn was found in her Bangor, Maine, apartment. A Robert P. Inman of Holden, Maine, was arrested for speeding on June 26 and taken to the Bangor Police Department where his right palm print was recorded. The print matched one found at the scene of the crime and he was subsequently indicted for the elderly Ms. Dunn's murder.

Extraordinarily, at the time Bernard assumed the identity of Robert Peter Inman, a Robert P. Inman was incarcerated in the Penobscot County Jail in Bangor, Maine, a mere two-and-a-half-hour drive from the Northern National Bank in

Mars Hill where Bernard had recently begun his odyssey.

The Charlotte Dunn murder and Robert P. Inman's subsequent arrest, incarceration, trial, and conviction were a sensational news story in northern Maine that continued for many months. Esoteric legal challenges were brought by Inman's counsel alleging improper evidentiary procedures related to the palm print obtained after his arrest for speeding and a follow-up search of his person.

The substance of the legal conflict centered on Inman's palm print that his attorney argued was unconstitutionally obtained as a result of being stopped for a traffic violation, which his counsel maintained did not rise to the level of a crime. Inman had been an immediate suspect due to his previous involvement in a similar offense and based on his proximity to the murder at the time that it occurred. Interviewed a day after, he was released from custody because of a lack of evidence. However, a policeman began following him, and on June 26 he was arrested for speeding. Instead of issuing him a summons, Inman was taken to the Bangor Police Department where his palm print was recorded. Subsequent analysis indicated that it was a probable match with a print found next to the body of Charlotte Dunn.

Using the seemingly identical print as a basis, authorities obtained a search warrant to get all of Inman's prints and some hair samples as dark hair had been found grasped tightly in Ms. Dunn's hand. The evidence acquired from the search resulted in his indictment and was an essential part of the case against him.

The appeal kept his name and the murder in the news while it worked its way through the court system to the Maine Supreme Judicial Court. A consequential ruling denying his appeal was issued on March 13, 1973. Robert P. Inman was in the Penobscot County Jail throughout the process and was subsequently convicted of murder. Later, when domestic and international law enforcement officials identified Robert Inman as a possible person of interest regarding the Mars Hill bank robbery, the possibility that he might be the same person already in jail for Charlotte Dunn's brutal murder was the cause of substantial confusion. Bernard would be the serendipitous beneficiary of this unlikely occurrence.

For the present, Bernard would be traveling abroad carrying the assumed identity of someone with the same name as an incarcerated murderer near his home in Maine. Lunar, who had become a nightly lover and companion during his short stay in Southern California, would not be invited. He intended to tour Europe in search of new conquests. Momentarily disappointed, she too would quickly recover and move on with new replacements.

• 9 •

Trans Atlantic

*"He was very aware of his
sex appeal to women."*

—A friend

Friday, December 3, 1971, was a momentous day at UCLA. The UCLA Bruins men's basketball team began their season with a 105 to 49 victory over The Citadel. Their star center, Bill Walton, would lead them to an unprecedented undefeated thirty-win season. Coached by the legendary John Wooden, they would go on to capture the National Championship and superstar Walton would be selected college basketball's player of the year. Walton, known as the "world's tallest deadhead," was a seven-foot-tall enthusiastic Grateful Dead fan with an unconventional life-style that very much mirrored the counterculture of Southern California. He would become an iconic figure in university history; and both college and professional basketball. Ubiquitous campus fervor for the team spanned all political and cultural divides and served to unify the school, if only momentarily.

Bernard and Bruce were two of just a handful of people even distantly associated with the university that weren't particularly interested in the game. Other more immediate and compelling commitments were on their minds that Friday evening. The UCLA fall semester had ended earlier in the day and they were making final plans for a European ski vacation. Bernard had previously purchased two first-class one-way tickets on an Air France flight from Los Angeles International Airport to Paris via London. The departure time was 8:05 the following morning. Thoroughly distracted by his fling with Lunar and the perpetual party Bernard had been living, the need to purchase new luggage had been completely forgotten until late in the day. He had hurriedly rushed to the local White Front discount store and acquired two small Samsonite suitcases.

Only during the last minutes of packing did they realize that the two suitcases were too small to accommodate all of the still somewhat moist currency. Foregoing any spare clothes, they hastily crammed the suitcases full with cash. Still having remaining money to conceal, they stuffed the balance into their boots and clothing. Entering the airport terminal with just the clothes they were wearing, a couple of toothbrushes, and two suitcases filled with damp, stolen cash, they deceptively looked the part of a typical pair of young, privileged American tourists leaving on vacation. Perpetually smoking a cigarette, Bernard was relaxed and calm. Bruce was anxious—distracted with other issues on his mind. Cesar Chavez was in the midst of a historic, controversial United Farm Workers boycott that would impact his post–law school graduation plans to advocate for migrant workers. The spring school semester began on January 3. He was game for a party or several parties for that matter but after that he had goals to pursue. Bruce needed to be back at school by the end of the month.

As his passport indicated, Bernard was now traveling as Robert Peter Inman. The timing of his identity transformation was providential. On the evening of December 1, Assistant U.S. Attorney Kevin Cuddy in Bangor, Maine, had authorized a warrant for Bernard's arrest for robbing the Northern National Bank in Mars Hill. On December 3, his office publicly announced issuance of the warrant for his apprehension and an all-points bulletin accompanied by a blurred photo, and his description was circulated domestically and internationally.

However, most law enforcement officials continued to believe that Bernard was in Canada and that was the primary focus of their investigation. Suspected murderer Robert P. Inman was safely locked away in the Penobscot

County Jail in Bangor. No one was looking for Robert Peter Inman.

Airport security for commercial airline departures in 1971 was essentially nonexistent. There were no secured, safeguarded arrival and departure terminals, and other security precautions and screenings were minimal. Rummaging through passenger baggage or body searches during departures was almost unheard of without establishing a basis for probable cause. Bernard and Bruce simply walked up to the ticket counter, presented their reservations, and, carrying their suitcases crammed with money, self-assuredly proceeded onto the plane when boarding was announced.

Once in flight, Bernard relaxed in his seat by the window, ordered a glass of wine and lit up a Pall Mall. While he and Bruce enjoyed the comfort and benefits of first-class accommodations, which included almost uninterrupted flirtations with lavishly tipped stewardesses, Bernard reflected back on the past three weeks. An eventful period of time: he had robbed a bank, hidden out on a mountain for a week, traveled across the country, assumed a new identity, and was now flying to Europe with his good friend Bruce carrying about $90,000—all without getting caught. Accepting the unpleasant reality that he would eventually be apprehended, his principal goal was to have as little money left as possible when he finally was taken into custody. Although inconvenient and uncomfortable to carry, especially in his boots, his stolen treasure would have substantial buying power when they reached their destination as the exchange rate for the French franc was five and half francs to one American dollar and four to one for the Swiss franc. The possibilities seemed limitless; *if* they were successful in smuggling their concealed riches through French customs.

While imbibing in early morning drinks at a pub at Heathrow Airport in London during their stopover, Bernard had a chance encounter that would lead to romance and abundant benefits in the future. Sitting at the bar with Bruce, a stunning blonde British Overseas Airways stewardess entered and sat a couple of seats away. Statuesque, shapely, and *Playboy Magazine* beautiful with large gorgeous eyes, Bernard was immediately smitten. He was determined to meet her.

When the stewardess ordered a gin and tonic, Bernard had the bartender give him the check and ordered a second one for her. Waving delicately, she smiled and thanked him. Totally captivated, he promptly asked, "What flight are you on, where are you going, I'll buy a ticket?" Amused, she responded that having just returned from Rome, she was now off duty.

Adding that her plan was to have one relaxing drink and then catch a taxi home for a long, restful sleep. Two drinks was definitely her limit. Leaving Bruce, Bernard joined her. Much taller than him, Bernard was undaunted. He found her to be almost as charming and intelligent as she was beautiful. Her lovely blue eyes and smile were intoxicating. Bernard was madly in love.

Born in nearby Maidenhead a few miles west of London, Margaret "Maggie" Ward, age twenty, was the daughter of a prominent local physician. Two years ago after Maggie's mother died, she had decided to forego a university education and become a stewardess instead. Independent and adventurous, she wanted to see the world. Intrigued by this self-assured, handsome American with intense, piercing eyes on his way to a ski trip in the Alps, she found herself falling under his charming spell. Just as Bernard was inviting her to breakfast, Bruce interrupted to remind him that their flight to Paris departed in a few minutes. Maggie willingly gave him her phone number and address. He promised to call her once he was situated in Geneva. Perhaps she would visit him when a flight took her there, he suggested. She agreed.

Descending into Orly Airport near Paris, Bernard and Bruce counseled one another on dealing with French customs. They needed to look the part of innocent, unremarkable American tourists. If their suitcases were opened, there would be no acceptable explanation for two bags crammed full with weathered cash and absent any personal belongings. They would be in violation of a multitude of customs regulations and currency smuggling laws. Follow-up body searches would confirm the worst of their initial suspicions. Bruce would have some serious explaining to do and law school was likely to be put on hold or worse. Unbeknownst to Bruce, Bernard could expect extradition and incarceration for the foreseeable future.

Reassuring themselves, they reminded each other that this would be easier than dozens of days and nights they had experienced in the tunnels. No murderous Viet Cong bastards waiting in ambush to waste them; just a handful of relatively harmless French bureaucrats to contend with. They would pull it off and watch each other's backs, as they always had.

Double checking his fake moustache, walking was awkward for Bernard as he approached the customs checkpoint. He could feel the bulky, damp cash pressing against his feet and shins, crowding the inside of his Joe Willie Namath Dingo Boots. Cautiously trying to walk normal, more money was uncomfortably stuffed in his underwear and around his waistline. Selecting the line for those with nothing to declare, he calmly waited his turn. Staring at him with penetrating eyes, the inspector asked him something in French. Sounding nothing like the Canuck French his Canadian friends spoke, he didn't understand. Unruffled, Bernard placed his suitcase on the counter and negatively shook his head in silent response, simultaneously handing him his passport. Carefully scrutinizing Bernard while comparing him with the picture in his passport, they were a perfect match. Continuing his extended eye contact, the inspector slowly signaled for him to pass.

Stepping away from the inspection booth, he could feel money being forced up and slipping over the top of his boots. Peering down, a twenty dollar bill was falling out of the bottom of his right pant leg. Never looking back, he nonchalantly reached down and carefully wrapped the errant Andy Jackson in his hand then walked to a nearby rest bench. Seating himself, he pulled the boot partially off and forced the remaining cash back down inside. Unobtrusively glancing around the area, no one seemed interested in his predicament.

His former platoon leader joined him a few moments later. Bruce had also been waved through without inspection.

The two tunnel rats were now free to roam in Europe.

• 10 •

Swiss Rats

*"(He) could display sybaritic tastes.
He could be down to his last ten dollars
with the rent coming due but he would buy
a T-bone steak and a bottle of Lancers
wine because he wanted it."*
—A friend

After surviving customs at Orly Airport in Paris, Bernard and Bruce encountered their first problem with travel on the European continent; the language barrier. Neither of them could speak French, a significant disadvantage in France. Bruce had absolutely no experience with the French language and Bernard was limited to a few words of Canuck he had learned growing up with the numerous French descendants living in northern Maine and nearby New Brunswick, Canada. Parisian French was virtually indistinguishable for him. They had difficulty reading signs and didn't understand what people were saying. Finally, a shrewd cab driver who was fluent in English adopted the inexperienced American tourists—for a fee. Bernard paid him handsomely to transport them to the train station and assist in buying tickets to their proposed skiing destination, Geneva, Switzerland.

Except for nearly missing an intercity train connection in Lausanne, Switzerland, after carelessly overindulging in local wines, their trip to Geneva was uneventful. Reaching the train station late afternoon on Saturday, December 4, they were relieved to find that although the city of Geneva is in the French-speaking sector of Switzerland, English is a common second language spoken by large numbers of its citizens and a majority of the many foreigners living there.

The language barrier at least partially alleviated, currency exchange was another potential impediment to acquiring their unofficial international license to party. Discovering currency exchange services at the train station, their first cash conversion was an enormous success as they procured four Swiss francs for each American dollar. That profitable transaction completed, Bernard and Bruce were further encouraged as the exchange employee didn't question the ragged, weathered condition of the bills. Buoyed by their good fortune, Bernard hailed a taxi and directed the driver to take them to the most exclusive, expensive hotel in the city.

The Hotel de la Paix on Quai du Mont Blanc

along the shore of historic Lake Geneva was the cabbie's choice. The elegant, landmark century-old structure with classical Italian Renaissance architectural lines overlooked the harbor, where the grandiose Jet d'Eau fountain propelled water nearly 500 feet into the air. On a clear day, imposing snow covered Mont Blanc, highest peak in the Alps, and could be observed in the distance towering above nearby Mont Saleve, located across the harbor to the southeast.

Wearing cowboy boots and corduroy jeans, the two former tunnel rats looked very much the part of young, unsophisticated American tourists quite obviously out of their element as they entered the elegant hotel with an extended prestigious history. Customarily the choice of lodging for well-heeled artists, foreign diplomats, international aristocracy, and European royalty for over a century, Prince Rainier and Princess Grace were only two of many notable visitors known to frequent the hotel. Bernard and Bruce would now be hobnobbing with some of the world's elite. They resolved to pretentiously assume the urbane role their current circum-stances allowed. Bernard speculated that he wouldn't mind meeting the gorgeous Grace Kelly during their stay.

Intent upon adopting polished, cosmopolitan appearances, the uncultured pair spent 3,000 francs on new wardrobes during their first full day in Geneva. Visiting an upscale hair salon, they departed stylishly groomed. Now they were outwardly prepared for Geneva, but were the Genevois ready for them?

A very proud, somewhat patronizing snobbish city, ancient Geneva can trace its history back more than 4,000 years. A banking and financial hub, it is perhaps most renowned as one of the world's most influential cities for global diplomacy. Home to numerous headquarters for various international organizations such as the Committee for the Red Cross and the World Health Organization, it is known as the "Peace Capital."

Ironically, the two former military warriors, one a fugitive bank robber, were staying at the "peace" hotel in the reputed peace capital of the world. Peace in Vietnam was still very elusive. On December 9, five days after their arrival in Paris, the Vietnam War Paris Peace talks collapsed. More than fifteen months of violence would transpire with thousands of additional military and civilian casualties before the United States would ignominiously end its involvement in Vietnam and another two years before the war would end. Arguably, all the suffering and expense incurred after more than a decade of war, and all that Bernard and his fellow soldiers and friends had endured, would be in vain. Peace was not an issue that consumed

Bernard. He had more hedonistic things on his mind.

With an estimated 40 percent of its population foreign born, Geneva was truly a global community. Not a place normally distrustful of foreigners, particularly those who were English speaking, it had a well-deserved reputation as being an exceptionally hospitable environment for expatriates, especially wealthy ones. Bernard and Bruce did not attract unnecessary attention or arouse the suspicion of Swiss authorities, at least initially.

Surrounded by two mountain ranges, the Alps and Jura, and at an elevation of over 1,200 feet, Geneva is a habitual recipient of snow in the winter. Higher elevations in the nearby mountains experience abundant amounts of snowfall, making Geneva one of Europe's great skiing destinations. Excellent skiing opportunities are nearby and some of the most prestigious ski resorts in the world are within a two-hour driving radius. A couple of adventurous "rats" now found themselves in a skiing paradise.

Bernard and Bruce frivolously squandered money on expensive food, clothes, and drink, especially indulging in copious amounts of booze. They ate at many of the city's most expensive dining establishments. Bernard's favorite restaurant, Auberge de la Mere Royaume, was one of the oldest in Geneva with an inventive menu that featured French classics, Swiss specialties and a refined, elegant Old World atmosphere. Formerly a connoisseur of cheeseburgers and French fries, Bernard discovered Genevois cookery and acquired a craving for the Swiss national dish, fondue bourguignonne. Refined addictions came easy for Bernard.

They dined on entrecote bordelaise and trout Grenobloise at the Auberge de la Mere Royaume, ate Coq au vin at the Perle du Lac by the lime and chestnut trees overlooking Lake Geneva, and sampled the flambé creations at Café Mozart. In just a short time, Bernard was ordering exquisite cuisine at the best restaurants with the confidence and superiority of a polished aristocrat.

Bernard promptly acquired another addiction: expensive wines. He preferred Burgundy and Bordeaux, having a particular predilection for Saint-Emilion.

Decades later, Bernard could still recite his favorite vintage wine years. They were 1952, 1953, 1959, and 1961 for Bordeaux and 1955, 1961, and 1964 for Dom Perignon. He once paid 740 francs for a single bottle of 1924 Chateau Lafite Rothschild. Later, when entertaining, he would buy out a restaurant's entire stock of 1959 and 1964 Dom Perignon.

The more lavishly Bernard spent money, the more he discovered about the art of spending it.

He pretentiously became what he aspired to be, one who personified affluence—someone who did not spend money to acquire power, status, or fame but rather he was the quintessential hedonist. In his first four days in Geneva, he splurged 4,000 francs on food and drink. Without the moderating influence of Bruce, he would have spent more.

While dining at the Auberge de la Mere Royaume, Bernard and Bruce became aware of the Fête de l'Escalade, an annual festival held in Geneva to celebrate the defeat of an attack on the city during the night of December 12, 1602. Inspiring wooden panels on the restaurant wall depicted scenes from that historic event. In fact, the restaurant derives its name from legendary Mere Royaume, wife of Pierre Royaume, born Catherine Cheynel. On the night of the military assault, the 60-year-old mother who had given birth to fourteen children was living above the town gate. Discovering the clandestine siege, she poured a cauldron of boiling soup on the attackers, killing one and alerting the sleeping residents. Held on the weekend closest to December 12 and one of the city's foremost spectacles, l'Escalade was celebrated on the first weekend after their arrival.

On Saturday, December 11, while nurturing a bottle of wine at a café overlooking the harbor with an intimate view of Jet d'Eau, Bernard and

Bruce first heard that the Fête de l'Escalade was actually being celebrated that weekend. The bartender and other customers talked of parades, various events, and a huge party in the Old Town. Anxious to experience l'Escalade, they left the Hotel de la Paix on Quai du Mont Blanc in search of festivities the following day. After walking across Pont du Mont Blanc, they hiked past English Garden, up Place du Port and Rue de la Fontaine into the heart of the Old Town.

They encountered thousands of celebrants swarming the streets of the Old Town when they arrived. The crowds were colorfully dressed, exuberant, and festive. Almost every block contained a small l'Escalade party of raucous merrymakers, well-fortified with mulled wine surrounding a great cauldron of boiling vegetable soup. Bernard and Bruce joined several of the gatherings as enthusiastic participants. Only a small amount of encouragement was required before they learned to fervently exclaim, *"Ainsi perisset les ennemis de la Republique"* (Thus perish the enemies of the Republic) after each robust gulp of mulled wine. While they were eagerly imbibing at one cauldron, an eccentric parade of several hundred garishly dressed revelers passed on its way toward the Cathedral St. Pierre. Appearing disorganized and chaotic, they eventually realized it was a formal promenade. Wearing historical costumes, some on horseback, and others carrying ladders in remembrance of attackers attempting to scale the walls of the city, there were drummers, musicians playing period instruments, and others carrying seventeenth-century weapons. Children in costumes were frenetically racing about throwing eggs at one another and dousing spectators with flour. Europe's largest historical parade, it was a bizarre and raucous event. The two tunnel rats were thoroughly entertained.

Later in the day, Bernard and Bruce met two young women visiting the Fête de l'Escalade from southern Switzerland. Both speaking fluent English, they spent the remainder of the evening together sampling soups, breads, and candies while continuing to consume generous portions of the omnipresent mulled wine. Bernard's companion was a dark, fascinating young woman named Mia from a small village near Zermatt at the foot of the Matterhorn. A mountain climber and avid skier, Bernard was intrigued with both Mia and her lifestyle. They discussed a possible skiing date in the coming weeks. Bernard considered inviting her back to the hotel but then recognized that although he and Bruce shared a relatively spacious suite, it was insufficient to meet his romantic needs.

At that moment Bernard concluded that it was time for a change. The luxurious Hotel de la Paix no longer met his expectations. The prospect of meeting Princess Grace had lost its glitter.

A small man with a big appetite, he required more space.

• 11 •

Last of the Rats

"Amongst his friends, people paid attention to him. They knew if he said something, it was important."
—Mark Carney, friend

After more than a week of unrestrained extravagance in Geneva, the two former tunnel rats turned bons vivants had yet to realize at least Bruce's primary purpose for traveling to Switzerland, skiing. Since Bernard was determined to find new lodging that better suited his perceived romantic needs, they decided to relocate closer to a major ski resort.

Villars-sur-Ollon, a renowned skiing destination seventy-five miles west on the opposite side of Lake Geneva, was their choice. Villars at an elevation of more than 4,000 feet is an idyllic Swiss mountain village situated on a southwest-facing plateau that towers over the Rhone River Valley and offers breathtakingly spectacular views of the alpine peaks of Dents-du-Midi and Mont Blanc in the heart of the Vaud Alps. From the center of town, hardy skiers can take a train to the famed ski area of Bretaye or a gondola another 700 feet higher to Roc d'Orsay. Starting at either location, a competent skier can travel all the way back down to the village. With scores of kilometers of ski trails including additional links to Gryon and other ski areas, Villars was exactly what they were looking for—a very luxurious vacation in a skiing Mecca. A host of gorgeous ski bunnies would complete their vision of the perfect storyline.

Foregoing bus or train transportation used by ordinary tourists, on December 15 the unceasingly pretentious pair hired a limousine to transport them, their new wardrobes, and Bernard's burgeoning wine collection to Villars-sur-Ollon where they checked into the Palace Hotel. Obtaining an expansive south-exposed suite with exceptional views of the surrounding mountains, Bernard felt much more at ease with the less refined surroundings in their new hotel that had a reputation for accommodating affluent guests of considerable notoriety such as tax evaders, art forgers, political exiles, and unemployed movie stars—all at an exorbitant room rate. Unbeknownst to hotel management, they could now include a fugitive bank robber to their list of dubious patrons.

Bretaye had been a pioneer in the commercial skiing business in Switzerland and had a storied skiing history. At the beginning of the twentieth century horse-drawn sleighs were used to transport skiers from the village to the high slopes. The railway to Bretaye was constructed in 1913 greatly facilitating skier access, and in 1936 Switzerland's first ski lift was built up the steep valley from the Col de Bretaye to the crest of Chaux Ronde at an elevation of almost 6,500 feet. Later that year, another lift was built to an even higher altitude on the nearby peak, Grand Chamossaire. By 1938, Villars and the ski slopes of Bretaye had become one of the preeminent resorts in Europe. Ski clubs thrived, numerous champion skiers were developed, and celebrities from all over the world were attracted to this exceptional winter wonderland. It was a vacation destination for the rich, famous, notorious, adventure seekers, and those that wanted to be. Bernard was a near-perfect addition.

Having previously frequented the slopes of Mount Baldy in the San Gabriel Mountains of Southern California at every possible opportunity, skiing enthusiast Bruce Hakala was thrilled to have his first experience in the Alps, considered by him to be the world epicenter for skiing. Bernard was encouraged. Since celebrities frequented Villars, meeting Princess Grace was still a possibility as she was known to be a regular visitor to the area. Unfortunately for him, she was almost always accompanied by her Prince Charming.

Bruce was an accomplished skier, Bernard was not. But he possessed an intangible trait that would be of significant benefit in the sport, virtual fearlessness. Renting the best equipment available on the first day after their arrival in Villars, Bernard took a lesson while Bruce explored the slopes. Characteristically pushing himself to his physical and mental limits, the training was a self-inflicted, painful introduction to skiing in the Alps for Bernard. Persevering for just one day, he lacked the temperament or patience for further instruction. After that, Bruce was his "on-the-slopes" instructor and Bernard the enthusiastic apprentice. It was a definite case of role reversal from their days in the tunnels when Bernard had been the undisputed authority. Not surprisingly, Bernard progressed rapidly and he was quickly able to ski the more difficult runs with relative ease and confidence, albeit lacking the polished finesse of a well-schooled expert.

From Bretaye, a network of trails branched out making it possible to connect with the adjacent ski area in Gryon, adding many additional kilometers of skiing opportunities and an assortment of more difficult, challenging trails easily allowing for a full day on the slopes. The skiing was truly phenomenal.

Excitement and adventure were two of the primary reasons Bernard and Bruce were there. They resolved to exploit all possibilities.

On most days, they arose late after a night pursuing women and either took the dramatic gondola ride to Roc d'Orsay or the picturesque train trip to Bretaye. From Roc d'Orsay there was a long expert descent passing through Bretaye to Villars. Although Bernard usually took a few sometimes near catastrophic falls on the upper section, this was his favorite run and he stoically accepted the bruising consequences of his choice. Bretaye offered an array of options varying from easy to difficult. They would spend several hours skiing on the slopes usually stopping for a respite of hot mulled wine at a little bar below the Col de Bretaye Restaurant sometime during the day. Their day on the mountain would end with a gentle descent to Villars, enjoying the expectation of another evening out on the town and the increasing hope of meeting that perfect girl or at least one who was willing.

While riding the gondola to Roc d'Orsay on their third day of skiing, they shared the ascent with the most beguiling skier Bernard had yet to encounter. Blonde and shapely with a scattering of light freckles on her cheeks, wearing a hot pink form-fitting ski suit, she was simply the most gorgeous woman he had met since arriving in Switzerland. Scandinavian in appearance, he attempted to charm her with compliments but she either didn't speak English or was feigning the same. Struggling to find someone in the gondola who could act as his translator, preoccupied with the spectacular views, no one volunteered. Resorting to embarrassing, futile attempts at sign language, the gondola strained to a halt at the top and she quickly exited.

Leaving Bruce and pushing past others, Bernard clumsily attempted to catch her while wrestling with his skis and poles. Before he could reach the lovely lady, she had donned skis and began her descent. Rushing, he fumbled trying to attach his boots to the bindings on his skis and valuable seconds were lost. Finally organized, he raced down the mountain only to lose his balance after less than a hundred yards; wiping out in a dramatic crash ending with a violent face plant. Lifting his head and brushing snow from his eyes, he caught one final glimpse of an ever smaller pink figure disappearing down the expert run. Arriving to help, Bruce was relieved to find that nothing was hurt but Bernard's pride: he was suffering the pain and disappointment of the gorgeous girl that had gotten away.

Villars provided yet another compelling attraction for Bernard: some of the world's finest wines were produced in the region. Located in the foothills of the Swiss Prealps, wine towns in the area cultivated grapes on terraced vineyards that resulted in exceptional Chasselas, Pinot Noir, and Gamay. Having a decided preference for reds, Pinot Noir was added to his ever-growing list of favorites. His latest addiction continued to flourish.

Their evenings were filled with the active night life that Villars and nearby Gryon had to offer. Numerous restaurants and bars kept them out until late each evening, and there was never a shortage of attractive, charming women— just a shortage of willing ones. Initially, their romantic aspirations went unfulfilled despite a substantial effort on Bernard's part that included utilizing all of his considerable easygoing charms and spontaneous generosity. Princess Grace was also a no-show. He placed calls to both Maggie and Mia. Neither was home or they didn't answer.

Failed attempts at meeting the opposite sex were almost too numerous to count. Buying drinks for unaccompanied women or a group at a table was their primary modus operandi. The result was many satisfied drinking women in the Canton of Vaud but no takers for the determined former tunnel rats. Taking turns with their advances, wagers were made on the outcomes. They were consistently losers in the game of love.

One night at a bar in Gryon, Bernard thought he'd struck gold. Having spent much of the evening plying a beautiful dark-haired Swiss woman with expensive brandy, he was just preparing to invite her back to the hotel when her very possessive, hulking boyfriend joined them. A threesome didn't appeal to him. Ominous prospects for a lonely winter seemed a discouraging possibility.

After several days of skiing and hard drinking, Bruce came down with a severe cold. Feeling miserable, bored, depressed with his circumstances, and trying to recuperate while restricted to the hotel room, the forced relaxation gave him time to reflect on his situation. It was December 20 and he needed to be back in school on January 3. At the moment, he was quite sick and until he was sufficiently recovered there was little he could do with the exception of contemplating his choices.

Unlike Bernard, Bruce had a fairly clear road map for his future. He was going to finish law school, and after graduation he intended losing himself fighting the cause of migrant workers. Naïvely hoping to forget forever the agonizing hell he had experienced in Vietnam, that was a quest he would never realize. Their Swiss party had been a stimulating, mindless escapade but it was time for him to return to Southern California. He hoped Bernard would understand.

Preferably, they would go back to the sunny West Coast together.

When informed of Bruce's decision to return to school, Bernard was uncomplaining but resistant. They discussed various options for Bernard to join him. But of course, unknown to Bruce, he was a fugitive bank robber and none of the suggestions was truly viable. Secretly, Bernard feared that returning through U.S. Customs with a false passport was a recipe for his arrest. In the end, a mutual decision was made for Bruce to return alone. Bernard would generously provide him with the necessary travel funds and an appreciative spring semester scholarship in the form of a sizable monetary gift. He would remain in Switzerland until he ran out of money or the law caught up with him.

They weren't sentimentalists, but parting was difficult for both of them. Theirs had been a perplexing, circuitous journey. Having experienced a veritable hell on earth that few others had shared, they had lived to tell about it. Bernard and Bruce were closer than most brothers. Implicitly and unconditionally trusting each other as neither had ever let the other down; they had saved one another's lives on several occasions. Few things in life were more important to Bernard than friends that he trusted.

The emotional bond between them was inseparable. Memories and nightmares of the horrors they had lived through together in the tunnels of Cu Chi would be an integral part of their respective psyches for the rest of their lives. Bruce was beginning to acquire a greater cognizance of that reality and trying to address it. Bernard was not. He would continue pursuing his own personal brand of escapism living a life of extreme decadence, burying his subconscious and himself in all the superficial pleasures his misbegotten wealth allowed.

Bruce's health improved and two nights later Bernard threw an impromptu party in the hotel bar to reluctantly celebrate Bruce's departure. Buying several rounds for all of the very grateful patrons, Bernard was quickly the center of attention in an establishment replete with ski bunnies. Several gravitated to him. Engaging in conversations with two very sexy, attractive Dutch girls staying at the hotel on extended vacation, the aspiring Casanovas had finally found the female companionship they'd so desperately coveted. Sophie and Lotte were simply looking for fun and excitement, skiing was of minimal interest to them.

Paradoxically, on Bruce's last night in Switzerland, he and Bernard had finally found willing playmates. Sophie and Lotte would provide a different version of the "Dutch Treat."

After spending an exquisitely wild and romantic night with Sophie, Bruce was sorely tempted to change his plans and remain in Villars. Bernard added to his dilemma reminding him that there was a lot of money left to spend. He and the two Dutch delights conspired to encourage him to reconsider. Summoning all of his willpower, he resolved to remain true to his plan. Bruce was adamant that he would be on the train to Geneva later that day, December 23.

Belatedly, Bernard had come to the realization that their lives were unalterably changing and the two of them were now moving forward in distinctly different directions. Although they would always be more than just buddies, Bruce's departure would probably be the end of their remaining closely connected. A very good chance existed that they would never see each other again.

They didn't.

Bernard found himself alone again. Not an unusual circumstance, he had often been alone in the tunnels of Cu Chi and the jungles of Vietnam. He had robbed a bank and escaped by himself. Having always survived in the past, he would now. But at least momentarily, he wondered how.

Of course, he had recently encountered two fun-loving, potential playmates from the Netherlands. Sophie and Lotte would be double the fun and Bernard, now known as Robert Peter Inman, was game for just about anything.

• 12 •

Decadent Rat

"Make Love Not War"
—Louis Abolafia

With Bruce gone, Bernard was faced with a dilemma, what to do next? And, who to do it with. He preferred staying in Villars where he hadmade some potentially helpful acquaintances during the short time he'd been in Switzerland. Perfectly located for skiing, he had developed sufficient skills to thoroughly enjoy the sport when not in pursuit of his favorite pastimes, wine and women. Being familiar with the locale and having recently met two seductive Dutch charmers who were still lingering in the Palace Hotel searching for more excitement sealed the decision.

Contemplating how to best preserve the attention and companionship of Lotte and Sophie, Bernard decided to rent one of the numerous chalets in the area and establish a more permanent, roomy lodging arrangement that might entice them to join him. Staying indefinitely would be an even better alternative. While converting cash and continuing to receive a very favorable exchange rate of four Swiss francs for one American dollar, he had established a casual friendship with a local banker, Jan Germund. Discussing his desire to stay in Switzerland for an extended period, Jan suggested renting a recently vacated chalet he owned on the outskirts of Villars.

They agreed on 1,200 francs per month rent for the comfortable three-bedroom chalet above the village. Within walking distance of the downtown area, it provided easy access to restaurants, bars, and the train station to the Bretaye ski area. Facing south and overlooking the Alps and Mont Blanc, Germund's chalet was the ideal location for Bernard's personal private party central. Inviting Lotte and Sophie for drinks and hopefully their affections on his first night in the chalet, they loved it and immediately moved in. With the company of two gorgeous ladies and having amassed a sizable wine collection, a euphoric Bernard had found the perfect antidote for the disappointment he felt over Bruce's departure.

Although they would occasionally ski during the day, the vast amount of the fun-loving trio's energies was expended drinking expensive wine, consuming fine foods, and debauchery. Bernard had the money and stamina to support their rapacious appetites and Lotte and Sophie the willingness. The former medal-winning tunnel rat and jungle warrior had found another endeavor at which he excelled; decadence. Quite ironically, he had accidentally adopted a life-style that epitomized one of the most popular slogans of the antiwar movement, "make love not war."

As the end of 1971 approached, Sophie suggested that they throw a huge, festive New Year's Eve bash at the chalet. Both Bernard and Lotte embraced the idea and the three party animals spent the remaining days of December recruiting potential celebrants in the bars of Villars and on the slopes of Bretaye. Their efforts were a colossal success and more than forty people appeared at one time or another. Employing a very casual approach, no formal invitations were extended and no body counts conducted. Just a succession of rabid party-goers who were intent on having one hell of a good time wandered in and out of the chalet through-out the entire evening. Bernard enthusiastically spent more than 1,500 francs entertaining them.

Sparing little expense in making the party an overwhelming triumph, Bernard served unlimited caviar and a seemingly infinite supply of Dom Perignon champagne vintage 1959. His affable personality and deep pockets attracted the attention of two very alluring young ladies who were visiting from England, Kate and Lucy. Ostensibly on a ski trip, like their Dutch counterparts, they were primarily in search of fun and adventure. The small handsome man from America with the devil-may-care demeanor intrigued them. Lucy had a compulsive fondness for caviar and an almost instantaneous lust for Bernard. They had extra space in the chalet, Bernard observed, inviting them to move in. For him, adding two new additions to his romantic feminine circle would provide the ideal way to ring in the New Year. Like wine, his hunger for new paramours was essentially inexhaustible.

Initially wary of his unexpected offer, Kate and Lucy demurred. Moving in with the obvious suggestion of cohabitating with two completely unknown women and a reckless man with a seductive smile seemed like a dubious proposition fraught with possible hazards. Conversely, both had impetuous libertine inclinations and a strong sense of adventure. They agreed to give the proposal additional thought. Sophie suggested the five of them have a post–New Year's Eve party late the following day when they had recovered from the current one. Everyone concurred.

The New Year's Day party turned out to be a realization of Bernard's loftiest expectations. The unconventional quintet was compatible in almost all respects; good food, wine, and sex being their priorities. Skiing was just an occasional distraction. The possibilities were far too tempting for the two formerly reluctant English ladies with a daring sense of adventure. Relenting, they moved in the following day. Bernard had found the precise opposite of the filthy gruesome life in the tunnels of Cu Chi. This was his definition of heaven on earth.

Spending the days lounging at the chalet or skiing on the slopes, the frolicking five usually enjoyed their evenings sumptuously dining and drinking in the restaurants and pubs of Villars. Bernard and his four lovely companions were easily the most unusual and conspicuous members of the local night scene. With Bernard equally attentive and considerate to all four, he lavished each of them with affection and their favorite, most expensive food and drink. Appearing to be an odd, carefree bohemian family collectively attached by lust, Bernard was the envy of many and a source of awe and amazement to others. Quite unbelievably, his circumstance would soon change even more dramatically. He would transition from an abnormal arrangement to bizarre.

Taking the train to Bretaye for a day of skiing, Sophie and Bernard encountered two stunning young women from Canada on the ride up. Students on an extended ski vacation, Camille was a willowy brunette from Quebec City while Ghislaine, her tiny doll-like companion with short nut brown hair, originated from a small town near St. Georges, Quebec. Both lived only a few hours from Mars Hill. French speaking, neither had a good command of English. Fluent in both French and English, Sophie quickly assumed the role of translator. This was their first visit to Bretaye and the two lovely ladies from Quebec sought guidance on the slopes and the night life in Villars. They too were primarily seeking amusement and pleasure.

While Bernard and Sophie would be the perfect guides for both, Bernard wondered what if anything they knew about the bank robbery. Neither making any mention of it and seemingly unaware of the crime, he was cautiously relieved. Still, he would carefully avoid any reference to his Mars Hill connection.

The foursome enjoyed a full day of skiing that included an extended respite in the pub at the Col de Bretaye Restaurant, imbibing in a local favorite, Vin Chaud, a hot mulled wine. Similar to one of their favorite winter drinks in Quebec, Camille and Ghislaine enthusiastically consumed several. Unable to complete the ski descent to Villars due to their tipsy conditions, they took the train. Before departing, they agreed to meet for dinner at the Hotel Central Restaurant in Villars, one of Bernard's preferred eateries.

Hotel Central specialized in fondues and nothing satisfied Bernard's emerging gourmet palate like fondue bourguignonne. Small chunks of steak dipped in a communal hot oil sauce, he found the local Pinot Noir to be the best wine to accompany his favorite dish. Using a fondue fork to dip the small pieces of sirloin steak into the large pot of steaming oil, when someone accidentally dropped a piece into the pot, they conscientiously adhered to the timeless Swiss tradition associated with eating fondue. If lost by the man, he bought a round of drinks, and, if by a woman, she kissed each of her closest companions. Recipients of several affectionate kisses and copious amounts of Pinot Noir, Ghislaine and Camille were quickly enamored with Bernard and his coterie of lovely, playful diners. Extending a dinner invitation at the chalet for the following night, they readily accepted.

The two engaging Canadian lovelies were immediately fascinated with the situation at the chalet, an obvious perpetual love fest. However, having some prudish misgivings, they resisted Bernard's initial invitation to join them. Further, six women to one man seemed like poor odds in what was for them a completely unfamiliar living arrangement. Otherwise, this wild bunch with a lavish lifestyle and wonderful accommodations had much to offer, a never-ending party being the most obvious benefit. Plying them with exquisite food and all the Vin Chaud they could consume, Bernard was transparently trying to tempt them. Still, they resisted.

Jan Germund had previously turned Bernard on to a very exclusive, illegal gaming house in the nearby city of Montreux. Obtaining the necessary connections and password for admittance to the secretive establishment, Bernard hired a limousine to transport the potentially lucky seven gamblers for a night of wagering Northern National Bank's money. Losing a couple of thousand francs while having a deliciously clandestine and exciting evening, Ghislaine and Camille decided to give the madcap chalet and its insane inhabitants a trial run. Amazingly, they were now seven; six enchanting ladies and Bernard. It was a remarkable, improbable beginning to 1972 for him.

Returning in the limo after an evening of carefree gambling, a mildly inebriated Bernard reflected back on a much different gambling experience he had had in Vietnam just a little over four years before. He and some of his tunnel rat buddies had been involved with a cutthroat Vietnamese gambling operation and he owed them over 4,000 piasters. They'd threatened him and others. Deciding to deal with them his way, he had placed a substantial C-4 explosive under their hooch. Detonating it while still much too close, the concussion blew him down over an embankment. Dazed but unharmed, he crawled back up to find the hooch and all occupants completely destroyed. In the world according to Bernard, he had performed a service for humanity. He did not like being threatened.

Military and Vietnamese investigators concluded that Bernard was a probable suspect in the execution-style explosion. Vietnamese officials wanted to interrogate him. In accordance with standard military procedures at the time, when an American soldier had legal problems with a foreign government, the army shipped him back to the United States rather than expose the serviceman to a foreign judicial system and possible imprisonment. Reassigned to Fort Hood, Texas, he would later tell friends that he was the "only soldier ever kicked out of Vietnam." Though not precisely correct, it was close.

Declining to report for duty at Fort Hood, he wandered around Texas for a few weeks before signing in. When he did, the army wanted him back in Vietnam. Lightly punished for his illegal absence from duty, his unique skills had been sorely missed. He arrived in the Imperial City of Hue just in time for the Tet Offensive. Hiding out in the jungle by himself until the massive campaign which would have a lasting impact on future American conduct of the war subsided, he then joined his new unit the 101st Airborne Division.

When out on the town celebrating, the seven unrestrained partiers attracted an unusual amount of attention. A young American man apparently dating six gorgeous women simultaneously and spending lavishly on them, while they doted on him, was difficult to miss. Bernard was single handedly turning Switzerland, the diplomatic capital of the world, into his own personal Sodom and Gomorrah.

Nothing attracts men like beautiful young women and money. A swarm of eager adoring male worshipers were soon in hot pursuit. The six ladies and Bernard were joined by three men; an Italian, an Austrian, and another Dutchman. Generous under most circumstances, Bernard drew the line at three guys. There was a definite limit to how much he was willing to tolerate and share. The chalet on the hill had become an international house of parties.

The ever-growing commune continued to live an existence of exceptional extravagance and indulgence regularly feasting on Scotch smoked salmon and lobsters. Extraordinary drinking bouts of incredible proportions and expense were almost the norm. Parties would continue day and night with participants joining in, resting or pairing up with partners for extracurricular entertainment. Bernard frequently spent as much as 1,200 francs in a day for fine cuisine and excellent wines.

Bernard acquired a taste for raclette, a traditional, indigenous Swiss meal. A melted cheese dish, it was an expensive specialty of the Col de Bretaye Restaurant. He would gather up anyone in his entourage who was interested and take the train to Bretaye to savor raclette cheese melted in front of an open fire. Sufficiently warmed, the browned cheese was scraped onto their plates and served with specially cured ham, dried beef, pickled vegetables, and small boiled potatoes. While spending several hours luxuriating in the dining experience, they would sip chilled bottles of Pinot Gris. If able after overindulging themselves, they would ski down to Villars. Usually, they took the train.

Bernard and Lotte purchased small pans and a grill sold specifically for preparation of raclette dishes and experimented with their own concoction. Nothing compared with the exceptional gourmet meal served by the restaurant on top of the mountain, so that idea was discarded.

His exorbitant spending continued at an incredibly foolhardy pace. Bernard had an expensive stereo system installed in the chalet ensuring that loud music blared from the house of parties almost continuously. He commissioned a renowned silversmith named Lombard from Geneva to make him an opulent silver bracelet and a jade ring. With the assistance of his personal Dutch wardrobe experts, Lotte and Sophie, he went on another shopping spree splurging thousands, adding to his collection of new clothes.

With the assistance of Jan Germund, he invested 16,000 francs and purchased a half-interest in a small restaurant in Malaga, Spain, sight unseen. Since Spain did not have an extradition treaty with the United States, he schemed that he might move there after he ran out of money. He could live off the business profits, possibly making enough money to repay Northern National Bank. Assuming he didn't get caught first.

Days of excess turned to weeks. Warmer winds and longer days were signs of impending spring. Seasons were changing but the perpetual, promiscuous party went on unabashedly. Casual visitors came and went taking advantage of free everything: food, drink, and sex. One brief guest was of particular interest to Bernard, Jack Scott, a Canadian from Toronto, Ontario. Both having a fascination for fast cars and faster bikes, they contemplated exploring the Alps on motor-cycles in the spring. Scott left for England the next day.

While on a flight layover in Geneva, stewardess Maggie Ward spent a night with Bernard in the chalet. Although normally quite broad-minded, she was astounded by the heavy, around-the-clock drinking and unrestrained sexual activity. Counseling him that the lifestyle was harming his health, she suggested he leave it behind. Joining her in England would be a better alternative and one she would prefer, she insinuated. Promising to give her proposal some additional thought, he discussed obtaining her assistance in paying off a debt to his friend Brian Blanchard. Maggie assured him they could work something out.

Bernard was thinking about home.

• 13 •

Homesick

*"He trusted Ed. He challenged him
in a positive way."*
                    —Dottie Wheeler

A daring warrior and cold-blooded killer when
he needed to be, there was a softer and gentler
Bernard. Although he had a hardscrabble, dirt
poor childhood, he always had a warm spot in
his heart for home. The greater Mars Hill area
was where his roots were. Located in Aroostook
County, the northernmost and geographically
largest county in the State of Maine, people
from the "county" have an almost universally
held perception of themselves, one shared by
many others. Uncommonly tough, hardworking,
independent, self-sufficient, and unabashedly
reticent, they are uniquely bonded by a common
culture, homogeneous demography and a
relatively inhospitable environment for nearly
six months out of most years. Bernard was a
"county boy" through and through and forever
would be.

Except when he was in the army, Bernard had

spent his entire life in northern Maine. Whenever he finished a tour of duty in Vietnam or went on leave, he was always flush with funds acquired in the black market. He could have gone almost anywhere in the world that he wanted. Instead, a motivated, inner compass always navigated him home.

While having the time of his life in Switzerland living large with more money than he'd ever dreamed and a house full of gorgeous women, something of more significance was missing. He had a void that needed to be filled, a subconscious connection that required nurturing and replenishment. Resisting the obvious, he was homesick.

Bernard had a patently unusual relationship with Deputy Sheriff Edgar Wheeler. Although they had been on conflicting sides of the law on a few occasions, with Bernard involved in a variety of relatively small-time legal infractions prior to the burglary and bank robbery, the two polar opposites instinctively liked each other. Bernard consistently drove his motorcycle too fast. Deputy Wheeler stopped him several times for speeding, reckless driving, and operating without a license. But instead of citing him for violations, he usually gave him warnings, both personal and official.

When staying with his uncle Grover Patterson in Bridgewater, Edgar and Dottie Wheeler had lived next door. The relationship between

Bernard and Edgar evolved into a genuine friendship. Becoming close enough so that Edgar was comfortable allowing him to ride their horses, it was a thoughtful gesture extremely valued and appreciated by Bernard. In Dottie's words, "He trusted Ed. He challenged him in a positive way." For Bernard, Edgar was a respected older brother figure.

Curious about happenings back in Maine and missing home, in late March 1972, Bernard placed a long distance call from Switzerland to his only friend in the law enforcement community, Deputy Wheeler. The following conversation ensued:

Patterson: "Hello, Edgar? This is B.K. How ya doing?"

Wheeler: "Hello, Bernard. Where are you?"

Patterson: "Come on now, you know that's not a fair question."

Wheeler: "Okay. What do you want?"

Patterson: "I was just sitting here thinking I ought to tell you I invested all the money I took and I'll pay back the bank in a few years."

Wheeler: "When are you going to give yourself up?"

Patterson: "That depends on how much time I'll get."

Wheeler: "That depends on how much money you've got left, Bernard."

Patterson: "I don't have too much."

Wheeler: "How much did you spend?"

Patterson: "All of it. I told you I invested it."

Wheeler: "It might be hard on you. But
I promise you, I'll do everything I can if
you give up."

Patterson: "Well, then you're going to have
to find me first."

Bernard hung up. Deputy Wheeler later disputed that he had specifically asked Bernard how much money he had left but otherwise confirmed the balance of the conversation.

Bernard also called Edgar on several subsequent occasions. Contents of those conversations were never revealed. While not disclosing his whereabouts, Bernard consistently asserted that he would return to Mars Hill and make things right. Edgar always encouraged him to surrender. Despite the bank robbery and his involvement in other illegal activities, they remained guarded friends. Bernard respected Edgar and held him in highest esteem.

On a warm early spring evening, Brian Blanchard received a phone call from his friend Bernard. He did not say where he was and Brian didn't ask. It was mutually understood that he was somewhere "overseas." In fact, Bernard was calling from Villars.

They exchanged greetings and then Bernard

related, "I'm doing good. You know the $100 you loaned me? I'm going to pay it back. I have a stewardess friend over here who will get the money to you."

Swapping the friendly banter of long-time friends who had once unexpectedly met in Vietnam, they debated whether or not Bernard owed $50 or $100. Brian insisted the correct amount was only $50. Bernard was even more adamant that it was $100. That was what he was sending, he asserted, and hung up.

The next day while hanging out with friends in Al's Diner, Brian mentioned his phone conversation with Bernard the night before. News, especially about Bernard and the bank robbery, traveled fast in Mars Hill. A few days later, two agents from the FBI showed up to interview him. Brian told them everything that had transpired during their conversation and added that Bernard wasn't a bad guy. Blanchard asked what he should do if he received the money. They didn't have an answer.

Despite his numerous romantic liaisons after the robbery and escape, Bernard still had a strong affection for his girlfriend back home in Maine. With the assistance of his cultural advisor, Sophie, he purchased a Paris original for 1,200 francs while shopping in Geneva and shipped it to his sweetheart in Maine. Unfortunately, customs refused its passage. It never reached her.

Later, he called his girlfriend on a couple of occasions. He carefully avoided mentioning Sophie and the other five women sharing the chalet with him.

Bernard and his circle of irresponsible companions were not living in a social vacuum. People were beginning to notice their extravagant, outrageous lifestyle. Neighbors were upset about the loud music and neverending party. Their libertine behavior offended others. Even some of the hard-partying ski crowd was annoyed, although much of that was envy. Complaints were filed with the police. Bernard had attracted unwanted attention.

• 14 •

Cornered Rat

"Bernard did not suffer from a lack of hubris."
—A friend

While Bernard continued to party hearty in Villars, back in Maine scant progress was being made by the FBI with their bank robbery investigation. No good leads had been developed and the prevailing presumption continued to be that Bernard was hiding somewhere in Canada. A fugitive warrant with his photograph and a description had been circulated worldwide. However, the picture was somewhat faded and no one was looking for Robert Peter Inman.

In Villars, Bernard had attracted the attention of the local Swiss police. Following up on complaints about wild lavish parties, loud music, and erratic excessive spending, a police detective visited the chalet and interviewed Bernard. Apologetic while denying any mis-behavior or the allegations of raucous noisy parties and other disturbances, he promised to make a concerted effort to ensure there were no future problems. Evasive regarding personal questions and the source of funds that supported his profligate spending, the skeptical detective left obviously dissatisfied and suspicious.

Characteristically, Bernard didn't panic. Essentially unperturbed, he gave no consideration to flight. Much more dire circumstances were necessary before he would contemplate that option. Immediately returning to his irresponsible lifestyle, he remained in his international house of parties with its conspicuous collection of revelers. With Bernard continuing to finance their extravagant, promiscuous behavior, very little changed except they were now more visibly restrained and less outwardly ostentatious.

Persisting with their investigation of Bernard, determined authorities in Villars discovered a technical violation of local tax law. He had not paid his taxation du jour, an obscure infrequently enforced daily tax levied on renters. An officer was dispatched to deliver a notice of demand for payment of the tax and a written explanation as to why he shouldn't be fined for noncompliance. Bernard and Sophie were skiing when the police official arrived at the chalet. An unconcerned, flirtatious Ghislaine happily signed acknowledging receipt of the notice.

Lacking insight into Bernard's hard-barked personality, village police didn't understand that he was not a person easily intimidated. Certainly not about a matter as insignificant as paying a tax he'd never heard of and apparently one enacted to charge him for simply breathing the air while renting Germund's chalet. Regardless, Bernard didn't pay taxes. He didn't owe society, any society anywhere, anything. In the world according to Bernard, he was all paid up. He ignored the notice.

Frustrated and distrustful, Villars police officials decided to take further action. Bernard was summoned to appear at the police station at 9:00 a.m. on March 27, 1972. He was ordered to bring his passport with him. While he could feel threatened when surrounded by a large contingent of heavily armed Viet Cong in the tunnels and jungles of Vietnam, unarmed, courteous Swiss police serving comparatively benign pieces of paper did not intimidate him.

Self-educated on how to survive, Bernard could effectively cope with the most egregious circumstances. The strategy he had perfected in Vietnam was to carefully assess every aspect of the surrounding happenings and environment, formulate a scheme to deal with the issues, and remain hypervigilant yet calm at all times. Interjecting healthy doses of bravado and confidence didn't hurt.

Once while tracking Viet Cong with his black Lab in the jungle west of Hue, he had observed a line of ants crawling in the sand along the narrow path on which they were traveling. Noticing an incongruent gap in the procession, someone or something had disturbed the industrious insects' otherwise regimented work habits. Moving silently, the two of them crept upon a company of substantially equipped North Vietnamese soldiers organizing for an attack. He and his dutifully muted canine friend stealthily blended into the dense vegetation. Shortly after, he called in a napalm strike with precise coordinates just a few hundred yards away from where they had taken hidden refuge. Much of the enemy detachment was horrifically incinerated in the ensuing bombing raid. His well-developed survival instincts had saved his life many times. Bernard would now utilize those same skills to address his current, much less menacing predicament.

Assessing the presumed police game plan, Bernard was convinced the summons was a ruse to see if he would overreact and take action that would betray him. If any solid evidence existed, they would most certainly have arrested him, he surmised. Deciding to treat the police as if he was back in Vietnam and they were the enemy, he would not allow them to dictate the terms of the game. Instead, to the extent possible, he would force them to play by his rules.

Bernard did not appear for the 9:00 a.m. appointed deadline. Instead, accompanied by

Lotte and Ghislaine, he staggered into the station at 3:00 in the afternoon apparently suffering the effects of a long night of celebrating. Apologizing for the delay, he announced that he had misread the summons and had forgotten his passport. Having disarmed his adversaries, Bernard then took the offensive. Demanding legal justification for the summons, a full explanation of the basis for the tax assessment and what any of that had to do with his passport. The police lacked immediate answers.

Unprepared for his requests and fearing they might be guilty of overreach, the officials relented. Bernard and his two lovely, gregarious companions departed without providing the police with anything they had required.

A day later, police again served a summons. This time, they delivered it to Bernard personally. He was ordered to appear at 9:00 a.m. the following morning with his passport. The stated justification was that he had failed to pay a tax mandated by local statute, and, according to Swiss federal law, a foreign citizen was required to present his passport to a duly authorized law enforcement official whenever requested.

Changing tactics, Bernard appeared as ordered. Once more accompanied by coquettish Lotte and Ghislaine, who were intentional distractions, he again failed to bring his passport. It had been misplaced, he explained. Promising to contact the American Embassy immediately for a replacement and stating that he wanted to appeal the levy of the taxation du jour, police repeated their prior negligence allowing him to depart without obtaining any of the requested information. Contacting the American Embassy was not on Bernard's "to do" list.

Although the criminal bulletin received by the Villars Police Department was lacking in details and failed to include a photograph, it provided a brief description of a wanted fugitive, Bernard K. Patterson, who was being sought for robbing a bank in the United States. The depiction appeared to fit Robert Peter Inman, a troublesome tourist who had become something of a local legend for throwing riotous parties and reckless, wasteful spending. A photograph of the dubious, annoying Mr. Inman was needed to share with American officials.

Police again summoned Bernard to the station. Requesting that he pose for a picture since he'd lost his passport, he cheerfully obliged. Bernard was not that naïve. Suspecting another motive, he still believed his fake name and new moustache would protect him from being identified. Transmitting the photograph through the Swiss Foreign Service Department to the United States, they asked for confirmation of receipt and instructions on what actions they should take if it was determined that Inman was the fugitive wanted for bank robbery.

In a happenstance of incredible good fortune for Bernard, the police request was completely bungled. Due to bureaucratic mishandling, the photograph and written request were both lost. Never received by the FBI, Swiss officials did not get a response.

Although they had found nothing of substance to justify their cynical suspicions, Villars police officials were convinced that there was something nefarious about Bernard. Contacting the Swiss diplomatic service for advice, they were informed that there was insufficient justification to initiate deportation proceedings. Deciding on a slightly different tact, they resolved to assert a claim that he was undesirable and demand that he depart the country without invoking any formal legal process. In short, they would intimidate him into leaving.

Receiving a written request from the police to vacate the country immediately, Bernard predictably resisted. Enlisting the assistance of his landlord, Jan Germund, an influential local banker and businessman, he appealed. Germund, who was receiving 1,200 francs a month in rental payments for his chalet, stridently objected to their proposal. With Germund vehemently characterizing police actions as harassment of a law abiding American ski tourist, the police backed down. Tourism was a significant portion of the local and Swiss economy. This sort of unilateral unjustified action could result in very adverse publicity, Germund had asserted.

Free to party, Bernard chose to ignore the ominous warnings that were beginning to swirl around him. He and his unwitting companions blatantly returned to their roguish behavior.

A week later, a German Swiss friend very secretively brought him perilous news. While at a police station in Zurich, he had seen a wanted poster for someone named Bernard Patterson hanging on the wall that looked exactly like him. Reaching the unmistakable connection, his friend predicted that it was only a matter of time before copies of the poster arrived in Villars.

Bernard deduced that his days of safely celebrating in Villars were numbered. His grand vacation experiment had come to an end.

Placing a call to Maggie Ward in England, he confided that he was ready to accept the invitation to join her if that was still an option. Assuring him that it was, she promised to adjust her work schedule so that she could take a couple of weeks off and show him around southern England as soon as he could catch a flight across the channel.

When did he expect to arrive, she inquired. Tomorrow was his unhesitating reply.

Gathering with his entourage of merrymaking friends in the chalet, Bernard confessed that he was in trouble with the law. While cryptically avoiding the details of his crime, he acknowledged that the police were believed to be closing in on him. The party was over.

Amidst household pandemonium and tearful angst on the part of some of the disappointed young ladies, Bernard quickly packed his bags. Ensuring that all of his remaining cash was secured and concealed in his luggage, he stoically left in a cab without further delay. His saddened followers would now have to fend for themselves. Their meal ticket had left. This was cause for some real tears.

Within a half hour of Bernard's departure from Villars, two Interpol agents were knocking on the chalet door. Responding, Sophie informed them that she had never heard of a Bernard Patterson but they were welcome to search the premises if they desired.

Finding nothing except six beautiful young women, three male companions, and an astonishingly large supply of wine, the agents collected as much information as possible from the uneasy inhabitants about the recently departed Robert Peter Inman. His former companions knew very little about Inman except that he had left earlier in the day and there was no one remaining who could pay the rent. They had very little information to offer and no one had ever heard of Bernard Patterson. A photo of him circulated by the agents only looked vaguely familiar they thought.

While fearful of the law, no one was inclined to say anything that might harm or betray their friend. Their knowledge was limited to very basic information they informed the investigators. He was a young, wealthy American who liked to drink, spend money, and ski occasionally. Although he had often mentioned California, they had no specific details about where he'd lived in the United States before coming to Switzerland. He hadn't said where he was going. He was a very private person, they collectively agreed.

Preoccupied with their own problems, difficulties belonging to Bernard or the law weren't particularly important to the recently deserted occupants of Germund's chalet. Their overwhelming concern was that they would soon be homeless.

Smoking a Pall Mall cigarette and sipping a dry martini while flying over the English Channel, Bernard reflected on another flight he'd taken just two years prior. Returning to Vietnam for what was to be his final tour of duty, he had just finished extended military leave in the Mars Hill area. After living his youth in abject poverty, having lots of money to spend while vacationing in his hometown had been a very satisfying experience. He had started dating a local girl and bought another brand new Corvette Stingray. Living the high life had come easy for him.

Returning to Vietnam had not necessarily been a difficult, negative experience for him. A dangerous environment when you didn't know your way around, he'd learned how to endure and flourish in that lawless place with no rules but survival of the fittest. It was like he'd imagined Dodge City to be in the old west. The man with the fastest gun and the shrewdest instincts was the hero. And, there was money to be made if one was enterprising enough.

He had found it compelling, almost addictive, to be out in the jungle or down in the tunnels by himself. It was also much safer to be alone because he didn't have to deal with anyone else's stupidity, Bruce Hakala being the exception. A natural woodsman, Bernard had found the jungle was little different than the Maine woods. Hunting down the Viet Cong like they were partridge was his modus operandi. Not relying on anyone and trusting only his primal instincts, he would pounce on the enemy and make the kill when they were most vulnerable. Or meld into the jungle if the danger was too great. The worst "bad ass" of all was not his self-assessment but that of those who knew him best. Yet, those who knew him best also called him a trusted friend and a "good guy."

Now he was traveling to a new destination with unique and different challenges, but he had a gorgeous woman waiting for him and lots of money to spend. Compared to Vietnam, this would be a cake walk. And everyone spoke English.

• 15 •

Royal Welcome

"(He) could be spontaneous in actions,
sometimes exhibiting risky behavior
almost flauntingly."

—A friend

Maggie Ward was waiting at Heathrow Airport when Bernard's flight touched down. Carrying luggage heavily encumbered with stolen money, he passed through United Kingdom Revenue and Customs without incident.

The two anxious lovers greeted each other warmly. Beginning their version of a honeymoon, they celebrated the reunion with several drinks at the same bar where they had met in December.

Having spent three months where French and German were the predominant languages, an English-speaking environment was welcome relief for Bernard. While he had adapted and developed sufficient linguistic skills to get by in Switzerland, universal English was a relaxing return to a sense of normalcy. For him, dealing with the minor differences in dialect and accent were insignificant compared to the almost constant mental exercises he had experienced trying to communicate in different languages. Bernard's very distinct Down East Maine accent was considered a charming novelty by most that he met in England.

Traveling in Maggie's new Triumph TR6, it was only a short drive from the airport west to the post town of Staines. Reminiscing about their romantic night in Villars as they enjoyed a relaxing ride on the motorway passing many notable, time-worn buildings and homes, they arrived at her flat in the quaint suburban Staines village of Laleham.

Addicted to speed and a sports car enthusiast, the Triumph was love at first sight for Bernard. The four-speed manual transmission, six-cylinder convertible was perhaps the best constructed vehicle ever built by automobile manufacturer British Leyland. Designed for aggressive driving in confined spaces, it could accelerate from zero to 100 kilometers in just over eight seconds and had a top rate of 190 kilometers per hour. The low center of gravity allowed for safer, more manageable high-velocity traveling on narrow, winding English roads. Bernard was impatient to test its limits.

Maggie had no objections except there was one very significant obstacle that Bernard had already quite succinctly observed. Everyone drove on the wrong side of the road in England. There would be at least a modest learning curve even for the characteristically unintimidated Bernard, she suggested. He was ripe for the challenge.

After an almost sleepless night of intense lovemaking, Maggie drove Bernard to the neighboring village of Wraysbury to meet her father, a successful medical doctor. A moderately wealthy aristocratic practicing physician whose patients were primarily affluent friends and neighbors, Dr. Benjamin Ward could trace his family lineage to the British royal family. Immediately suspicious and disapproving of Bernard, the very tall, haughty Dr. Ward was coldly cordial. Bernard was the latest in a succession of male companions embraced by Maggie who were of questionable character and social standing, according to his pretentiously refined, condescending standards. Attributing the tawdry quality of her romantic attachments to her very ordinary career choice, he had strongly opposed most of her life decisions since his wife had died two years ago. Bernard didn't like him either.

The following day, Maggie embarked on her commitment to guide Bernard to the various tourist attractions of London and southern England. Bernard had his initial experience operating a Triumph on the trip into London. The busy motorway and congested city traffic was an ill-considered choice for his English driving debut. From his unfamiliar perspective, other cars were always in the wrong place, going the wrong way, and making the wrong turns. Barely avoiding several potentially catastrophic collisions in the extremely vulnerable little sports car, Bernard was unconcerned while Maggie feared for her life. Reluctantly, he agreed to postpone his next encounter with English traffic until a more rural, less traveled environment was located.

Beginning their excursion with a romantic stroll down Regent Street into Piccadilly Circus, the young lovers spontaneously took turns posing for pictures in front of the naked statue of Eros at the Shaftesbury memorial fountain. Originally intended by sculptor Alfred Gilbert to depict Anteros, a Greek god who represented mature, reflective love, the statue was a fitting tribute to the cultured, philanthropic Earl of Shaftesbury. Instead, as time passed, it became known as Eros or Cupid, the god of more frivolous, sensual passion. Paradoxically, Eros was better suited for the nearby neighborhood of Soho and certainly more accurately mirrored the relationship between Bernard and Maggie. Ending, in their minds, the longstanding debate about the intended direction of the statue's erection, they ensured it was aimed straight at them for their photographs.

Continuing on to Wardour Street, the two attentive lovers immersed themselves in the music, night clubs, and erotic culture of Soho. Finding amusement in the many bars and titillating sex shops, they were frustrated in their wishful attempts to catch performances by famous entertainers who were known to frequent the district such as the Rolling Stones, Elton John, or the Kinks. Disappointed, they drank away the remainder of the day enjoying less renowned performers who were equally talented, simply suffering from relative obscurity.

Next on their sightseeing agenda was a visit to one of the world's most famous and mysterious sites, Stonehenge. Traveling west and driving through the quintessentially English communities of Hook and Sutton Scotney, they arrived at the Bronze Age prehistoric monument in Wiltshire two miles west of Amesbury.

Spending about an hour touring the archaic site and contemplating the purpose and intent of the immense standing stones, Bernard was less than impressed. The concept of ancient peoples struggling for decades to construct huge monuments to commemorate the deceased and speak to their gods offended his very logical, pragmatic thought processes.

Bernard did not clutter his mind with spiritual matters, and from his viewpoint burial grounds were simply a place to dispose of the dead. In his short life, he had seen countless dead people, several dying at his hands. Frequently, enemy casualties were unceremoniously dumped into truck beds and transported to mass graves. American soldiers were usually stuffed whole or in parts into body bags and shipped home as quickly as possible. At the peak of the Vietnam War, the number of American combat deaths sometimes averaged more than 100 per week. Few if any had received special recognition or memorials. No need for elaborate shrines for anyone was Bernard's hardened, unsympathetic opinion.

Only vaguely aware and generally unsupportive of the antiwar protest movement, Bernard sometimes wondered if his privileged counterparts who were able to avoid the war and now expressing righteous outrage were actually suffering from a huge collective guilt trip. His opinion had been one shared by many of his fellow soldiers. Very few rich, pampered bastards had suffered and died with them in the tunnels and jungle. Most were in college protesting something. That was a simple fact in the world according to Bernard.

Leaving Stonehenge, they drove south to explore the bars and nightlife of the nearby historic community of Salisbury. After many drinks, Bernard took the wheel of the Triumph during their late-night return to Staines. Intent on putting it through the ultimate road trial, he would bury the speedometer needle on the tiny sports convertible. Quickly bringing the velocity up to 150 kilometers per hour, they heedlessly hurtled down the empty, twisting, narrow, dark country road. Approaching a relatively straight stretch of highway, Bernard determinedly pushed the accelerator to the floor as Maggie called out the ever increasing speed. Just as she screamed that he had exceeded the maximum level of 190 kilometers per hour, they topped a small hill.

The wheels left the pavement and they were abruptly airborne. Taillights barely visible, a slow moving vehicle was traveling in the same direction just ahead. Lightly hitting the brakes when they landed, Bernard methodically attempted to regain control of the careening car. Radically fish-tailing back and forth while barely holding the road, Bernard calmly nursed the steering wheel with measured, compensating adjustments as they rapidly approached the seemingly stationary vehicle directly in their crosshairs. Just before slamming into the rear end, he violently jammed the brakes. Whirling around completely backward, he brought the Triumph to a screeching halt. Ending in a ditch miraculously upright, the vehicle was undamaged.

Physically unharmed, Maggie bolted from the vehicle and vomited in the gutter. If the tiny convertible had hit even the smallest impediment while skidding sideways at high speeds, they would have flipped, instantly decapitating and crushing them both. The low center of gravity, the rack and pinion steering, and Bernard's cool, controlled responses had saved their lives.

While concerned and hypervigilant throughout, Bernard had remained calm and mentally in command. He had survived much more hazardous encounters on a regular basis in Vietnam. With no enemy trying to kill him, it had been just him and the Triumph against comparatively minor obstacles. It had been a relatively insignificant problem in Bernard's universe.

After pausing for several minutes to regain her composure, Maggie insisted on taking the wheel. Not lost on her was the fact that while Bernard's driving skills and subdued demeanor had saved their lives, he had been the primary reason their safety had been in jeopardy. Also quite obvious was her complicity in the near tragedy. She had willingly turned over the keys to him and supported the misguided adventure.

In the following days, Maggie escorted him to many of the most famous tourist attractions in the greater London area including the Tower of London, Windsor Castle, Hyde Park, Big Ben, and Trafalgar Square. Not a history buff and generally an indifferent sightseer, Bernard was far more interested in frequenting the pubs and taverns they would inevitably visit after each excursion. His favorite part of each day was the end when he and Maggie would wrap themselves around each other for an evening of impassioned sex. In that, Maggie was a willing accomplice. Dr. Ward would not have approved.

Much more pleasurable for Bernard than sightseeing were country rides they shared traveling through the Cotswolds in the Triumph. A range of rolling, pastoral hills replete with picturesque towns and villages, the Cotswolds were located in a region west and northwest of Stonehenge. Many of the distinctively British homes, public buildings, and ubiquitous churches had been built with their own Cotswold stone, a yellow limestone.

Choosing rare sunny days to traverse the almost 6,000 square kilometer region, they would select a different sector on each trip always ending the day at a pub in one of the upscale communities that dominated the area. When they were unable to curb their appetites and delay lovemaking until their return to Laleham, there was always a nearby bed and breakfast.

If they did return immediately after an evening of heavy drinking, Maggie always insisted on taking the wheel of the Triumph. No more nightmarish episodes flirting with death for her.

After a fortnight of living large with Maggie in England, Bernard developed an acute sore throat. Suspecting a cold, he initially ignored the condition. The soreness worsened and spread so that much of his mouth and throat was raw and very uncomfortable. Yet, there were no other symptoms of a cold or any other apparent illness.

Maggie encouraged him to see her father. Having acquired an immediate dislike for the imperious, sanctimonious doctor, Bernard declined.

However, the discomfort intensified. More frustrating, the accompanying foul breath was negatively affecting his love life, a completely unacceptable circumstance for Bernard. Finally, under ever more pressure from his now less sexually responsive lover, Bernard relented and requested an appointment with the arrogant physician.

Subjected to substantial lobbying by his daughter, a displeased Dr. Ward reluctantly agreed to see him. Cursory inspection of Bernard's mouth and throat revealed what was obvious to the doctor. Bernard was suffering the effects of excessive alcohol abuse. The doctor's disgusted, derisive diagnosis was alcohol poisoning. Bernard needed to stop drinking and take better care of himself, he asserted. He should return to the United States and join Alcoholics Anonymous was the doctor's sarcastic, yet hopeful prognosis.

Ignoring the pompous physician's clearly derogatory recommendation, Bernard decided on his own self-prescribed therapy. He would temporarily stop drinking and just smoke pot until the symptoms dissipated.

Both now on the wagon, the cannabis smoking honeymooners decided on a trip to the Isle of Jersey where the Ward family owned a cottage on the ocean. Maggie had spent many happy summer vacations visiting the island in her youth. Sharing that magical place with her new beau was a very intriguing prospect for her.

Driving southwest to the coastal community of Portsmouth, they took the day-long ferry ride to the Isle of Jersey. Located just fourteen miles from the Cotentin Peninsula in Normandy, France, and almost 100 miles from Great Britain, the largest of the English Channel Islands was seemingly an incongruent part of the United Kingdom. A significant player in the protracted, checkered history of conflict between France and England, the island had inexorably become linked to Great Britain over time despite its proximity to France. The Ward family had acquired their impeccably located coastal property in the nineteenth century.

Disembarking at the island's only significant city, St. Helier, it was just a short drive to the family cottage on Victoria Avenue overlooking St. Aubin Bay. A relatively small, yet extravagant home with a long sandy beach on the bay directly across the street, the two lovers began their second honeymoon. For several days, the sweethearts smoked pot, walked the almost empty, soft golden sand beach, bought fresh fish daily from the local seafood store, and made love, a lot. In a state of near domestication, for once Bernard was living an inconspicuous, relatively anonymous lifestyle.

March was a great time to be on the Isle of Jersey. Possessing a temperate climate year round due to the warming influence of the maritime environment, the temperatures were consistently in the mid-sixties during the day throughout their stay and it seemed like the sun was perpetually shining on their south facing lodging. After two weeks of searching for the ideal honeymoon environment, they had found it on Isle of Jersey—a remarkably idyllic romantic encounter for both of them.

Reminding Bernard of coastal Maine, he acquired an instant, consuming attraction for the scenic, majestic island. With agriculture and fishing the principal sources of income, the classic working fishing villages could have been Jonesport or Corea on the Down East coast of Maine. Bernard would have stayed indefinitely. Unfortunately, Maggie's cousin unexpectedly arrived with her family. The little cottage wasn't big enough for a party of six, especially for two lovers seeking privacy.

After their return from the Isle of Jersey, Maggie announced that she had used up her vacation time and had to return to work. She was required to contact British Overseas Airways and determine her new flight schedule immediately.

Enthusiastically encouraging Bernard to remain in her flat while she was away on work, Maggie enticed him with an added incentive— promising him use of the Triumph whenever she was gone. Assuring Bernard that there would be ample time to see each other when she was between assignments, she also tempted him with the possibility of making arrangements so that he could join her on some flights. Maggie wanted him to stay. Despite his sometimes reckless, erratic behavior, perhaps because of it, she cared.

A fugitive bank robber with his picture posted in public buildings around the world, the prospects of flying in and out of a variety of foreign countries on commercial airliners with Maggie did not seem like the wisest strategy to the former tunnel rat. A better choice seemed to be lying low in England and enjoying the benefits of his contraband wealth.

Maggie's first flight assignment was a trip from

London to New York and back. Secretly fearing possible exposure and arrest when passing through U.S. Customs, Bernard declined to join her. However, he had a special debt to repay and needed her help.

While Bernard was blatantly carousing around southern England and the Isle of Jersey with Maggie, the international search for him was gaining at least unsteady momentum. The Interpol agents who had just missed him at the chalet in Switzerland suspected that there was a connection between Robert Peter Inman and the bank robber Bernard Patterson. Securing a copy of his photograph from Villars police, they forwarded it to FBI officials in Washington, D.C., along with additional information they had obtained during their investigation. Included in their communication was speculation that the elusive Inman had probably flown to England shortly after his departure from Villars. They would await instructions.

FBI Headquarters in Washington forwarded the information to their agents in Bangor, Maine, and other local law enforcement departments. Everyone was mystified. Almost universally known in the Maine law enforcement community, the notorious Robert Inman was incarcerated in the Penobscot County Jail in Bangor for the rape and murder of elderly Charlotte Dunn. The old, faded photo they had on file of Bernard Patterson did not clearly resemble the likeness of Robert Inman who had recently been in Switzerland.

Time elapsed while attempts were made to sort out the investigatory dilemma. If the Robert Inman in Switzerland was in reality Bernard Patterson, why would he assume the name of a known infamous rapist and killer?

American officials wavered, Bernard and Maggie frolicked, and Interpol waited.

Unfortunately for Bernard, the honeymoon was over. Alone most of the time and still flush with stolen cash, he was bored. Boredom was his least favorite state of being.

• 16 •

Robin Rat?

"He was always a person of contrasts.
He had no good role models growing up."
—A friend

Despite his unmistakable abject self-indulgence while on the lam, Bernard had a generous sympathetic quality to his complex, often misunderstood personality. While he loved having money, a source of self-esteem that was very important to him, he knew better than most from personal experience what it was like to be financially destitute. A willful bank robber and hardened killer in combat, he possessed a charitable, sometimes compassionate facet to his complicated temperament that was less evident. Still, it was also a part of who he was, along with the inherent contradictions.

Given the poverty that Bernard had lived through during his youth, he displayed a surprisingly generous nature not just with those close to him but sometimes with complete strangers. Sharing his meager belongings with siblings, friends, and people in need had been an unlikely aspect of his hardscrabble childhood experience. Conversely, he could be miserly and selfish.

Very guarded with his thoughts and emotions, intimacy was something almost alien to him. However, his obvious strong affection for his grandmother was very apparent to many who were close to him. In a secure, private setting, he could share feelings of compassion and personal pain with a very small, select audience, but never in an even remotely public environment or with a group of peers. Having a limited but genuine capacity to reach out to others, he could also be very inconsiderate and quite self-absorbed.

Enigmatic is perhaps the most accurate description of his convoluted, uncompromising persona. Bernard could be exceptionally generous yet sometimes completely egocentric. Unusually understanding in one circumstance, he could be entirely mercenary and merciless in another. He eluded a simple uncomplicated characterization.

Returning home on leave from Vietnam well-supplied with dubiously acquired cash, Bernard spent it extravagantly on friends and family. On one of his extended visits, he purchased a canoe and an assortment of top-of-the-line fishing and camping gear. Refusing to acknowledge the government's authority to regulate fishing, he didn't trouble himself with the inconvenience of obtaining a fishing license. Embarking on a canoe trip down the famed Allagash River in northern Maine with his brother, it was an epic voyage. Experiencing bad weather, whitewater accidents, lost or damaged gear, and finally a runaway canoe, he embraced the misadventures and thoroughly enjoyed sharing his newfound wealth with his brother. For him, the high cost of the expedition and subsequent losses were inconsequential. The purpose of money was to spend it was his unapologetic view of finances. He was equally adept at obtaining it, illegally.

Undoubtedly, some of his conspicuous generosity was driven by pretense and a need to feel self-important. But another motivator was a genuine inclination to help those in distress. So it was not uncharacteristic for Bernard to readily share proceeds acquired from the bank robbery with others. This was particularly true if he perceived someone was suffering a serious problem or struggling with a financial hardship, especially if it was one to which he related. When that occurred, he would often spontaneously respond with assistance.

While on the run from the law and preoccupied with his impulsive, peripatetic lifestyle, he still found the time and energy to think about his longtime friend Brian Blanchard. Continuing to owe him $100 by his accounting, the liability weighed on him. He felt obligated to settle the debt. When Maggie returned to work with British Overseas Airways and departed for the United States, he gave her the money with instructions on how to transmit it to Brian once there.

Shortly after first meeting Sophie in Switzerland, she intimated that her lifelong ambition had been to form an orphanage. Having grown up an orphan, she knew first-hand the struggles that accompanied life as a parentless child. Although not technically an orphan, Bernard spent extended periods of his youth separated from his parents. Sympathetic, the idea intrigued him.

Despite their hedonistic, promiscuous behavior, possibly partially driven by it, the pair of would-be philanthropists contemplated establishing an orphanage and actually explored various possibilities. One of the motivating factors behind Bernard's decision to purchase an interest in the restaurant in Malaga, Spain, had been to use it as a means of achieving this goal.

Speculating that the restaurant could provide him with sufficient income to support his own needs and possibly fund a home for underprivileged children, he had suggested the two of them might eventually move there together. Since long-term thinking wasn't a hallmark of Bernard's normal behavior, this was indicative of another remarkable trait he possessed: he could be extremely calculating.

Although unknown to Sophie, forming an orphanage was clearly not an endeavor that Bernard could pursue in a location where he was perpetually subject to arrest and extradition. If the concept of an orphanage was going to become a reality, he needed to relocate to a relatively secure environment. Spain did not have an extradition agreement with the United States, making it an appealing place to spend his future.

His hasty retreat from Switzerland had at least temporarily put the orphanage idea on hold. Given their abrupt separation and his race to stay at least one step ahead of ever-encroaching international law enforcement officials, the prospect of an extended relationship with Sophie was probably history. But the worthy objective of founding an orphanage as a haven for needy, parentless children was still one that continued to fascinate and inspire him.

Perhaps Maggie would like to move to Malaga, he pondered. A sobering reality, Bernard lacked a sense of commitment or loyalty to the women in his life. While being involved with a woman was essential to his self-esteem, generally one was as good as another. More than one relationship at a time was completely acceptable, often preferable. Paradoxically, he could be very possessive and frequently jealous.

Arguably, his decision to flee to Maggie in

England instead of escaping to Spain with Sophie would turn out to be the wrong one. Certainly operating a restaurant and trying to establish an orphanage with Sophie in Malaga could have resulted in a dramatically different outcome, perhaps altering the remainder of his life. Years later, Bernard would often reflect on that possibility.

In Switzerland, he had intentionally lost 2,000 francs gambling. While playing a game of craps at his favorite clandestine gambling casino in Montreaux, he encountered a ski instructor that he'd previously met while taking lessons on the slopes of Villars. The clearly despondent young man had recently struck a young girl with his car causing significant injuries. Desperately seeking some semblance of atonement, he wanted to win the necessary money to pay for her hospital expenses. In direct competition with one another, Bernard threw the game. With buoyed spirits, the elated ski bum quickly departed with sufficient money to help his victim.

Waiting at the airport in Zurich for his flight to England, Bernard was distracted by a distraught woman who related a heart-rending story about being separated from her young daughter. Due to dire financial circumstances, she had recently been forced to leave the little girl with her sister's family as she was no longer able to support the child. Probably remembering his own youth, he secretly slipped 1,000 francs into her purse when she wasn't paying attention.

After dropping Maggie off at Heathrow Airport for her British Overseas flight to the United States, he met two Irish girls who were stranded in London without any money. Destitute, they were unable to buy airline tickets so they could return home to Ireland.

Having exhausted all known options, they didn't know where to turn for help. After buying them drinks and obtaining their addresses and phone numbers, Bernard charitably purchased their tickets and saw them off on a flight to Dublin.

Sporadically sharing his stolen money with people in need, Bernard was something akin to a twentieth-century version of Robin Hood. Like the outlaw from Sherwood Forest, he was not easy to portray or define and possessed almost mythical qualities. Distinguishing fact from fiction, legend from reality, and altruism from self-serving motives was and is an inexact process resulting in imprecise conclusions. A social chameleon, Bernard was different things for different people. Whatever his reasons, he did use some of the stolen money to help others. It did not appear to trouble him that the source of his beneficence was illegally obtained.

In early April, Brian Blanchard received a letter postmarked Grand Central Station, New

York, with no return address. Enclosed was a postal money order for $100 addressed to him. No other names or identifying information was included.

Suspecting it was repayment of the loan he had made to Bernard before the bank robbery, Blanchard immediately called the FBI. Contacting the agents who had previously interviewed him about the recent phone call from Bernard, he dutifully reported receipt of the money order. They never responded. After waiting longer than he deemed necessary, Brian cashed it.

The failure of the FBI to follow up on Blanchard's receipt of the money order was seemingly inexplicable. The investigation was open and active. Based on information recently provided by Interpol, the FBI and local law enforcement was puzzling over the possibility of Bernard having escaped to Europe using the false name of Robert Peter Inman. Normal procedures would have warranted further interrogation of Blanchard coupled with a careful examination and forensic analysis of the correspondence. None of that ever happened.

A pattern of investigatory ineptness on the part of the FBI seems to have emerged. Acting Police Chief Fay Fitzherbert, the first law enforcement official to arrive at the scene of the bank robbery, was never interviewed. Although Bernard had grown up living and playing in and around Mars Hill Mountain and was an experienced hunter and jungle fighter, a thorough search of the mountain area was never instituted after the robbery. People who had known him intimately for his entire life were never questioned. Now, while he was living out the role of Robin Hood in England, the FBI appeared to be a comic collective rendering of a bungling Sheriff of Nottingham.

• 17 •

A Greek Tragedy

"When in Europe his attitude was he had lots of money and was going to spend as much as possible before he got caught. Party as long as possible."
—Mark Carney, a friend

After an extensive interview with rapist and murderer Robert Inman at the Penobscot County Jail in Bangor, Maine, it was quite apparent to FBI officials that there was no connection between him and the bank robber Bernard Patterson. Collaborating with local law enforcement, the collective opinion was that it was feasible but unlikely that the Robert Inman in Switzerland was actually their man. Simple logic seemed to dictate that it was extremely unlikely that Patterson would adopt the identity of a notorious local sociopath whose name had been prominently in the news during the months leading up to the robbery.

The FBI notified Interpol in Switzerland that it was possible that Inman might be the Mars Hill bank robber but doubtful. They requested additional personal details on Inman enabling them to conduct a more comprehensive investigation in the United States. Interpol responded by providing everything acquired during meetings with the Villars Police Department and the results of their interrogations with the occupants found in the chalet.

Interpol also informed Scotland Yard in London to be on the alert for an American named Robert Inman, who was considered a possible robbery suspect. However, since the circumstances were not deemed high priority, the notification wasn't accompanied with any specific warnings or potential concerns. Given the relatively benign nature of the Interpol communication, no search for Inman was instituted by British officials.

* * *

His mouth and throat recovered, Bernard was drinking again, heavily. Living alone in Maggie's flat when she was away, which was most of the time, he was thoroughly bored. He began frequenting local bars and pubs.

Bernard's intolerance of boredom was legendary among those who knew him well. Having a very active mind, he craved diversity and was compulsively driven to stay perpetually busy. Alcohol and pot were his primary sources of relaxation. As one friend very succinctly stated, he was never going to be a nine-to-five employee.

Living out the role of a fugitive bank robber better suited his frenetic, risk-taking personality. While suspecting that law enforcement might be closing in, Bernard didn't have a sense of imminent danger. Unafraid and having more money to spend, he intended to party until it was completely exhausted or he was finally apprehended.

A compulsive gambler, Bernard habitually engaged in various games of chance with some of the resident bar flies while on his own in England, acquiring a host of regular gambling companions. Loving the thrill of gambling and even the risk of losing, he could sit for hours betting on which way hardboiled eggs would roll or spend an evening throwing darts wagering serious money on the outcome. In just a few days, he became a popular fixture in the local taverns.

Lonely for female companionship and confident of his natural appeal with the opposite sex, Bernard began using his innate charms to advantage. He started picking up women at bars, usually taking them to Maggie's flat. On one occasion, Dr. Ward observed him chauffeuring one of his dates in the Triumph. Unimpressed, his suspicions about Bernard had been validated.

On a warm, sunny day in April, Bernard had a fortuitous encounter that changed his plans dramatically. While driving Maggie's sports car on the outskirts of London, a very animated pedestrian flagged him down. The mystery man was Jack Scott, a Canadian acquaintance from Toronto that he had met at one of his parties in Switzerland. Renewing a conversation that began at the chalet in Villars, they discussed the idea of touring through the Alps on motorcycles.

Nearly broke, Scott was initially doubtful about the prospect. Bernard sweetened the bargain promising to buy bikes and fund the trip. They would drink, womanize, and gamble their way across Europe, he proposed. Having previously heard about the Greek island of Ios where nudity, overnight camping, and continuous partying were prevalent, he suggested that should be their final destination.

Having nothing better to do and in need of a meal ticket, Scott was still skeptical but willing to consider the scheme. A plan began to materialize. First on the agenda, buy the bikes.

England was home to some of the world's finest motorcycles. Triumph Engineering in Meriden, West Midlands, manufactured a much-sought-after line of Triumph motorcycles. Their latest model was the 1971 Trophy 500 (T100C). Designed for long-distance traveling on and off road, the Trophy 500 was an instant success and wildly popular. Bernard purchased a new one for himself and another used Triumph 650 in excellent condition for his traveling companion.

With images of *Easy Rider* in their minds, they would be the European version of Captain America and Billy exploring the road in search of drugs, free love, and adventure. The wannabe road warriors were ready to ride.

Saddling up with traveling packs that included Bernard's still sizable stash of stolen cash, the adventure seekers departed Staines. Motoring east for a final visit to a couple of bars in Soho, afterwards they competed in a high-speed race to the ferry terminal in Dover. Driving several motorists off the road with their reckless maneuvers, Bernard won. Taking the short ferry trip across a very narrow section of the English Channel, they entered northern France at the ancient port of Calais without incident.

* * *

Bernard had left a note for Maggie stating that he would be away for a couple of weeks but providing no additional details regarding his plans. When she returned, not only did Maggie find the note but also substantial evidence that other women had been sharing her home.

Adding to the insult, her thoroughly disgusted father called to report having seen Bernard escorting another woman in her Triumph. She felt hurt, used, and betrayed. Dr. Ward was simply relieved that he was gone, hopefully forever.

* * *

In addition to being one of the most significant ports in France, Calais was a popular gambling community. Still flush with cash, Bernard was an enthusiastic player. The easy riders passed most of their first night on the continent wagering and losing Northern National Bank's money. Ever observant, Bernard was impressed that Scott was not the least bit reluctant to spend his money.

Leaving Calais, they motored to the historic city of Reims where champagne was king. After stopping to sample and buy some of the region's best sparkling white wines, they continued on to Geneva. Bernard brazenly decided to spend the night in Hotel de la Paix, his first place of lodging when he and Bruce had arrived in Switzerland in December. Unsuccessful with attempts to contact any members of his former harem in Villars by telephone, they moved on the following morning. Bernard's inability to reach his former playmates was a most fortunate occurrence as they had been instructed to immediately notify Interpol when and if they heard from him.

The nomadic bike riders were an unnerving surprise for notoriously aggressive French drivers.

Known for tailgating and taking offense when passed, they weren't prepared for the likes of Bernard and Scott. Elevating road aggression to a new level, they habitually passed other drivers with reckless abandon on hills and curves in the mountainous terrain. Winding through congested traffic while ignoring normal driving courtesies, street lights, and signage, they didn't hesitate to pass on the right. The two road delinquents embodied the bad boy cinematic reputation of easy riders.

Having spent several weeks observing distinctive Mont Blanc from the chalet in Villars, Bernard was determined to get a close-up view. Traveling the highways south from Geneva, they entered the French resort community of Chamonix at the foot of the majestic massif.

Surrounded by the immense peaks of Aiguilles Rouges, Chamonix was a destination for world-class skiers and mountaineers. While a heavy smoker, Bernard was a sometimes hiker who had completed a backpacking trip with a friend in Maine's Baxter State Park during the previous summer.

After finding a room in the city, he recruited a less than eager Scott to join him on a hike to Le Glacier des Bossons, one of the most spectacular glaciers in the Alps. Beginning near the summit of Mont Blanc, it descended for over eight kilometers before transforming itself into a raging torrent that continued down into the valley, flushing through the heart of Chamonix. Wine was available at a hut near the lower terminus of the glacier. Bernard had never experienced accommodations like that in Baxter State Park. After several glasses of Beaujolais, the tipsy trekkers encountered an unsteady return to the village.

The following day, they took the cable car to Aiguille du Midi, not just in search of mountain views but with hopes of meeting available women. Experiencing success with the former, they struck out with the latter. Having no luck in any of the many night spots in Chamonix that evening, the two losers in love departed the next morning. They were back in the hunt for excitement on the road and more importantly, female companionship.

Climbing rapidly out of Chamonix on a steep wooded highway, Bernard and Scott left the impressive peaks and glaciers of Mont Blanc behind. Crossing into Switzerland near the tiny mountain village of Vallorcine, they stopped to savor the exquisite alpine views. Racing down into Martigny Valley, numerous hairpin turns made for a riveting, heart-stopping descent.

In serious need of female affection, Bernard called Mia in Zermatt, whom he had met in Geneva during the Fête de l'Escalade in December. She would be home and looking forward to his visit was her immediate response. Scott was also in luck as Mia had friends who were anxious to meet a Canadian. The intrepid travelers were on the road again with Zermatt their next destination.

Traveling through the Swiss Alps along the Rhone River to Visp, they then raced recklessly south to the Village of Tasch. The end of the line for personal motorized vehicles, the road to Zermatt beyond Tasch was closed to private traffic. Parking their motorcycles at the Tasch Railway Station and carrying packs, they took the train shuttle to Zermatt where Mia and friends were waiting at her apartment on the south side of the village.

At an elevation of over 5,000 feet, Zermatt is situated in the midst of the highest peaks in the Alps. Located in the shadow of the Matterhorn, one of the world's most famous mountains, Zermatt is foremost a world-renowned tourist attraction. A Swiss native, Mia waited tables in a small restaurant for two purposes: sustenance and the opportunity to play in the mountains. She was a hardcore outdoor girl.

An accomplished mountaineer and downhill skier, Mia had a different set of priorities than Bernard. Sex was not at the top of her list. A hike to the base of the Matterhorn was. Resigned to the unpleasant reality that their immediate needs were going unfulfilled, Bernard and Scott reluctantly agreed to a mountain trek.

After an exhausting day of attempting to keep pace with Mia and friends, the too-often-sedentary road combatants were finally rewarded with an evening of wine and romance. A familiar pattern began again. Bernard funded a continuum of heavy drinking, pot smoking, and promiscuous behavior.

* * *

In southern California, FBI agents had located Robert Inman living a life of squalor in a ramshackle beach house with several other drug addicts. Arresting him for various drug-related offenses, he was interrogated once coherent.

Suffering from withdrawal, the emotionally shattered Inman was no match for trained investigators. Quickly confessing to selling his passport to someone several months ago, he couldn't remember his name. His only recollection was that the buyer was a small guy about his size. Unable to find anyone who knew the passport purchaser in the drug-infested world in which Inman resided, it was evident that the person traveling with Inman's documentation in Europe was someone else, potentially the bank robber Bernard Patterson.

Interpol was immediately notified that whoever was carrying Inman's passport was a fraud and possibly fugitive bank robber Bernard Patterson.

In turn, Interpol sent alerts to authorities in all European countries. Since he was last believed to have flown from Switzerland to England, Scotland Yard began an intense search for Patterson.

* * *

After several days of partying in Zermatt, Bernard was anxious to continue to his exotic island destination in Greece. He encouraged Mia to join him. Employed in the restaurant and in love with Zermatt and the surrounding mountains, she declined.

Returning on the train shuttle to Tasch, they motored north to Brig and then traveled south crossing the border into Italy, continuing to the bustling, sprawling city of Milan. Unexpectedly, language and cultural differences were barriers to meeting women in Italy. Given their decidedly high expectations that they would soon have all the wine and women they wanted on the picturesque, temperate island of Ios, the two highway explorers persisted east across the northern part of the country passing through Verona and Venice to the border of Yugoslavia near Trieste.

Anticipating difficulty crossing into communist Yugoslavia, Bernard decided to employ a technique that had often worked in Vietnam: bribery. Assuming that border guards in the communist country were poor and corrupt, he purchased several bottles of expensive Italian wine. Their crossing was remarkably easy as the guards appreciatively accepted wine and cigarettes as an acceptable entry fee without further questions or scrutiny.

A long day of riding brought them to the drab, archaic city of Belgrade. After living the high life for several months in affluent Western Europe, Yugoslavia was a disappointment. Poverty and malaise seemed pervasive. Since the language was almost incomprehensible, they were relegated to a primitive form of signing to communicate. After spending two nights with prostitutes while hanging out in dingy night clubs, they were ready for the sunny, sandy beaches of the island of Ios.

Hurrying south, they had a one-night layover in the industrial city of Nis before arriving at the Greek border near Doirani the following afternoon. With just one more border to cross, they would soon be on their way to an island paradise.

Greek border authorities weren't so accommodating. In receipt of a recent bulletin from the Greek International Organization for Migration headquarters in Athens to be on the alert for an American named Robert Inman carrying a phony passport, they detained Bernard and Scott at the border crossing while awaiting further guidance.

Bernard's lifestyle and seemingly inexhaustible supply of money had been a source of trepidation for Scott from the first time they had met in Switzerland. As long as the money flowed his way without complications, he was fine. Now Scott wondered if he would be an unwitting accomplice to whatever crimes he'd committed.

The Greek bureaucracy couldn't have been more disorganized and incompetent. As a result of a comedic sequence of missteps and errors, they determined that there was no basis to arrest or hold Bernard. Rather, he was simply deemed an undesirable who was not welcome in the country.

Following instructions from Athens, the border guards denied Bernard and Scott entry and set them free, in Yugoslavia.

Depressed with their inability to reach their coveted destination, they retreated to the nearby city of Gevgelija. Finding a bar with attached rooms, they drank and smoked pot late into the night.

When Bernard awoke, Scott was gone. The Trophy 500 was also missing along with a small amount of cash he had left in his riding jacket. He was alone again. This time in the communist country of Yugoslavia dealing with people he didn't understand and signs and directions he couldn't read. But, he still had money.

Unafraid, Bernard recalled that he had been

alone in the tunnels of Cu Chi, tracking the enemy in the jungle and robbing Northern National Bank. Of one thing he was quite certain; he functioned best when alone, unencumbered by stupid people.

• 18 •

Desert Rat

"He craved excitement."

—A friend

Betrayed by Scott, an angry Bernard traveled north to Belgrade hoping to find him. Not in the habit of allowing transgressions against him to go unanswered, he fully intended to exact revenge. Scott was an exceedingly blessed man, and wily. Bernard was searching in the wrong direction.

Scott had returned to the Doirani border station and, unimpeded by Bernard and his phony passport, Greek border guards allowed him to enter the country. No dummy, Scott was now on his way to the island of Ios; he knew a good idea when he heard one.

Finding no sign of Scott on his trip to Belgrade or in the sleazy night spots they had previously frequented, Bernard realized his hunt for the thieving traitor was probably futile. Alone, he turned to the only person he knew in Yugoslavia, the prostitute Andjela, whom he had spent two nights with just a few days prior.

* * *

While at the post office in Staines, Dr. Benjamin Ward observed a wanted poster for an American bank robber named Bernard Patterson who was reputedly using the alias Robert Inman. The likeness was only vaguely similar. Not wanting to believe that he was the same person as Maggie's latest romantic interest, Dr. Ward carefully studied the fugitive's physical description. Almost identical to the Robert Inman who had been living with Maggie, he immediately contacted local police.

During his interview with police investigators, Dr. Ward described in detail the romantic relationship between Bernard and his daughter, disclosing everything he knew about the offensive Bernard Patterson. Providing them with medical records assembled when he had treated Bernard for alcohol poisoning, the outraged physician simultaneously expressed his professional opinion that Patterson had serious drinking and drug addiction problems.

When Maggie returned from an overseas flight, she wasn't quite so cooperative with interrogating officials. Decidedly vague and guarded in all of her responses, she carefully avoided providing any information about their travels or activities that might have assisted authorities in locating him. Although deeply hurt by his infidelities and abrupt unannounced departure, she still had feelings of affection for him.

Neither Maggie nor her father had any information or knowledge regarding Patterson's current whereabouts. Since he had left the Triumph TR6 behind, as far as they were aware, he had no known means of transportation.

After receiving a report from the Staines Police Department that they had located and interviewed his former girlfriend and her father, a prominent doctor, Scotland Yard informed the FBI and other European governments that the suspected bank robber Bernard Patterson was believed to be somewhere in England. Detectives were sent to Staines for the purpose of conducting a more thorough investigation and a local manhunt was initiated.

* * *

Communist Yugoslavia had little appeal for Bernard. Finding a pronounced shortage of fine wines, quality food, and lavish accommodations, he yearned for the halcyon days spent in France and Switzerland. While still retaining sufficient money with which to splurge, paying for women was an activity that offended his vanity.

Quickly tiring of Andjela and the gloomy surroundings in Belgrade, Bernard contemplated his next move. Based on his encounter with Greek border officials, it was apparent that his false identity had been compromised. Finding Yugoslavia confining and depressing, remaining in the communist dictatorship was not an acceptable alternative. Switzerland did not appear to be a viable option as he was fairly well known in several areas of the country. Flying out of the heavily guarded lightly used Belgrade airport seemed fraught with complications.

Short of remaining in Yugoslavia, any direction he went entailed a border crossing and potential risk of capture. Italy seemed like the best of several bad choices. Africa had always been a place that intrigued him. No longer having a road companion to negotiate with simplified decision-making, Africa was a possible destination after further exploring Italy.

Riding west to the Italian frontier north of Trieste, Bernard utilized the skills he had refined to an art form in Vietnam, reconnoitering the border area in search of weaknesses. Finding some old farm roads and herd paths in the notoriously porous boundary region northwest of Gorizia, he slipped into Italy unobserved.

Once over the border, Bernard was reminded of the difficulties he and Scott had experienced during their brief earlier visit. Encountering very few English-speaking people in a patriarchal society that was extremely protective of its young women, Italy was a difficult place to communicate and an almost impossible one to find the uninhibited girls he was seeking.

Bernard wandered around northern Italy for a few days, drinking their finest wines, sampling exquisite pasta dishes, and searching for feminine company. All attempts to meet the local girls failed. Reluctantly, he again turned to prostitutes.

* * *

His sex life in Vietnam had been a succession of prostitutes for Bernard. Incredible numbers of young, destitute Vietnamese girls, many abandoned by their families, congregated around U.S. military bases eagerly competing for the plentiful dollars the wealthy American soldiers were willing to spend.

An elaborate system of compensation evolved. Anything from a "short-timer," something as basic as oral sex in a village alley, to a week- or month-long arrangement could be negotiated. Generally accepted standard prices for the different relationships were established. However, like any commodity, the laws of supply and demand were the ultimate arbiter of cost. Prettier, bigger-busted girls demanded and received higher compensation. Absolutely any sexual activity or preference could be purchased, cheap.

A small town boy from northern Maine where prostitution was nonexistent, and a closet romantic, Bernard resented the system. Still he'd been a regular, enthusiastic participant. When he left Vietnam, Bernard resolved that he was finished paying for sexual favors. He failed miserably in Italy and Yugoslavia.

Finally, desperate for female affection, he called Maggie. Feeling sympathetic and protective yet still angry, she curtly informed him that police detectives had interrogated her and her father. They were now actively searching the area for him. Warning that he should not return to Staines and assuming that he was still in England, she suggested the Isle of Jersey might be a safe haven. She had not mentioned their island visit to the police. Avoiding disclosure of his location, Bernard apologized for his inconsiderate behavior, told her that he still cared and hung up.

Frustrated with his ongoing disappointments in Italy, Bernard needed a change. Now even more wary of a return to England, North Africa seemed such an unlikely choice that it might have the added benefit of deceiving those searching for him. He decided to ride south along the boot of Italy seeking a means of escaping to Africa. What he would do when he got there was a puzzling question that warranted additional consideration. He gave it very little. Instead, sensing that the law was closing in, he felt compelled to keep moving.

Motoring south near Bologna, Bernard was befriended by a local motorcycle gang. One member, Sergio, spoke marginal English. In need of English-speaking companions and information, he was quick with his generosity, lavishing food and drink on them.

Sergio was a veritable goldmine. Introducing him to one of the gang's groupies named Gianna, Bernard enjoyed a couple days of heavy drinking and tempestuous sex while supporting his new comrades in an extravagant fashion that they were completely unaccustomed.

More importantly, Sergio was a wealth of knowledge about the North African country of Tunisia. Having traveled there by motorcycle the previous fall, he had crossed the Mediterranean Sea by ferry from the Italian coastal seaport of Salerno to the Tunisian city of Tunis. Less than a day's ride south of Tunis was the island community of Houmt Souk, a tourist city with many French- and English-speaking people and an abundant nightlife by Tunisian standards. Just about anything could be obtained in Tunisia with money as bribery and corruption were a way of life there, Sergio added.

Leaving Sergio and friends behind, Bernard rode south past Florence, Rome, and Naples to the windy port city of Salerno in western Italy on the Tyrrhenian Sea. Stocking up with alcohol and cigarettes for both bribes and personal consumption, he purchased a ferry ticket to Tunis. Gale-force winds resulted in a very turbulent twenty-six hour ferry ride. Traversing the Tyrrhenian Sea between Sardinia and Sicily before crossing a narrow section of the Mediterranean and then entering the Gulf of Tunis, Bernard experienced his first bout with sea sickness. Almost constantly sick and vomiting profusely much of the time, he was more than enthusiastic to disembark in the capital city of Tunis.

Passing through Tunisian Customs was a charade that was easily resolved with copious amounts of wine and smokes. Instinctively, Bernard understood the benefits of his decision. No one would be looking for American bank robber Bernard Patterson in Tunisia; at least that was his version of reality. Conversely, Tunisia was not a desired destination for very many Americans, bank robbers or not.

The city of Tunis was an instant disappointment. Because most of the population was Muslim, accessibility to women and alcohol was very limited. The few available bars were filled with raucous patrons hurriedly gorging themselves with drinks. Unfortunately for Bernard, they were all men. Women were banned. How he could meet women in the rigid, restricted culture was a complete mystery to him.

Since Houmt Souk was highly recommended

by Sergio, Bernard quickly moved on. Riding south for a half day, he arrived at a significantly smaller, more cosmopolitan tourist community. Located on Djerba Island extending north into the Gulf of Gabes, he found many French- and English-speaking people. For Bernard, Houmt Souk was a notably easier place to play compared to Tunis, but still very repressive given the uncommonly libertine standards that he preferred and had grown familiar. The relative anonymity and protective cover that Tunisia presumably offered came with a high price for him: celibacy and temperance.

Houmt Souk didn't hold his interest for long. While sunning himself on nearby Houmt Souk Beach, Bernard encountered a local motorcyclist of French and Arab descent named Faris. From him, he learned of several adventurous bike rides into the Sahara Desert. May was an excellent time to ride in the desert as the temperatures generally stayed below 100 degrees Fahrenheit, Faris reported. Bernard eagerly agreed to join him for a trek to a remote oasis. If he couldn't meet any women, at least he would have some desert exploits.

Driving south for about 300 miles into the northern reaches of the Sahara Desert, the intrepid riders entered the oasis of Ghadames. Inhabited almost exclusively by Berbers, they lived a rough, primitive existence that was dictated by traditional rules of family dominance. Composed primarily of nomadic farmers, the oasis consisted of narrow streets, weather-battered mud buildings, and repugnant smells. Teeming with farmers, herdsmen, shopkeepers, dirty children, and low-profile women, Ghadames was a congested, busy marketplace in the midst of a huge intimidating desert.

Historically a combative people who adopted their own version of Islamic belief, the Berbers lived an uncompromising life in an unyielding environment. Bernard immediately liked and embraced them. What he didn't care for was the food. Beef lungs and sheep brains were a long dietary journey from the delicacies of Geneva or even a succulent American cheese-burger.

The Djerba Berbers of Ghadames farmed, bred cattle, and procreated according to ancient custom. A proud, male-governed culture, they called themselves Imazighen: man of noble origin. Women did the milking and gathering. Although women were not veiled and enjoyed more freedom than most Islamic cultures, their behavior was dictated and controlled by centuries-old family rules and traditions. Bernard quickly realized that any attempt to breach that societal chasm in order to meet the unattached women of Ghadames would be life threatening. Survival was a skill he'd perfected in the tunnels of Cu

Chi, and it served him well dealing with the mercurial Berbers.

Narrowly escaping his first day at Ghadames without getting into a brawl or worse, the defiant distinctly anti-Islamic Faris moved on— one step ahead of an equally belligerent and significantly more dangerous group of Berbers. Bernard had a new challenge in mind—testing his mettle against the elements furnished by the world's largest most intimidating, sweltering desert. Energized by excitement, he thrived on the emotional elixir of danger. The parched forbidding Sahara with sand dunes that sometimes rose hundreds of feet high provided a novel daunting outlet for the demons that drove his behavior.

After difficult, laborious negotiations with a local herdsman, Bernard purchased a camel and pack for $200. Leaving his Triumph 650 in trust with the elated seller, he galloped off into the seemingly endless sand dunes of the Sahara. Where he was going and what he would do was unclear—a distant oasis in Libya was his immediate goal.

The euphoric herdsman was convinced he'd consummated the bargain of his life. Having sold a flea-bitten cantankerous critter for an excellent price, he wagered that he'd never see the reckless American again. Instead, he would be acquiring a costly motorcycle without any effort or expense after Bernard almost certainly got lost and died in the desert.

Despite possessing substantial wilderness skills that had been undeniably proven in North America and Southeast Asia, Bernard was no match for the Sahara Desert. After only a day, he was hopelessly lost. Traveling in circles with every direction looking the same—nothing but endless sand dunes—he continued to mindlessly wander fully believing that he was destined to die of thirst or starvation.

Lying in the desert that night contemplating his predicament, he remembered pursuing Viet Cong in the darkness of the jungles outside of the Citadel City of Hue. Whenever possible, he had sought out the enemy at night, avoiding the light of day. Daylight was when the young West Point grads got themselves and their platoon members killed. Bernard had slept in the morning, smoked pot with the whores during the afternoon, and stalked the Viet Cong like he was hunting partridge back home in Maine at night. Back then, stealth and solitude were his biggest allies.

Later, rumors surfaced, possibly initiated by him, that he'd collected the ears of his kills in Vietnam and strung them up on a clothesline. When asked by a friend if it was true, he declined to answer. Speaking with his eyes, the questioner believed the answer was yes.

Although offering a much needed respite from the sun, darkness in the desert brought coolness, an intense sense of loneliness, and silent desperation for the completely lost former tunnel rat. Instead of the enemy lurking out there somewhere, there was something in many ways worse, nothingness. While unafraid, Bernard perceived no solution to his dilemma; his fate seemed sealed in the sands of the Sahara.

On the third day, having given up all hope of finding his way back to Ghadames, the routinely tenacious former warrior relinquished control of his circumstance to the mangy camel. This was the first good decision he'd made since leaving Ghadames. When it came to surviving in the desert, the outwardly stupid camel had far more desert sense than Bernard. Blessed with a remarkable homing instinct, the camel took charge and marched back to his stable in Ghadames.

While relieved to be accidentally returned to the oasis, the squalid desert community of Ghadames with all of its ancient rules and regulations had lost its attraction for Bernard. A world where sheep brains was haute cuisine, consumption of alcohol a punishable offense, and women untouchable no longer had any appeal. He was ready for civilization.

Despite the obvious hazards, Bernard resolved

to return to England and Maggie, the woman he now realized he cared for. He would leave immediately for the British Isles, dangers be damned.

• 19 •

When Irish Eyes are Smiling

*"He used sex as a badge of accomplishment.
He bragged of having sex with multiple girls."*
—A friend

Suspecting that she was withholding information, detectives from Scotland Yard focused much of their investigation on Maggie. Trailing her when she was home between flight assignments and watching her flat on a regular basis, Bernard Patterson was not observed and all of Maggie's activities had proved completely innocent.

After several days, detectives scheduled a follow-up interrogation. Their questions were concentrated on when and where she and Bernard had met, how they had spent their time together, and where they had gone. Because she was concealing information and in some instances fabricating statements, her testimony was replete with inconsistencies.

The interviewers knew she was lying and Maggie knew they knew she was lying. Still she bravely persisted with her conflicting stories.

Boldness was something of a newfound trait for Maggie. In that regard, Bernard had been a positive influence.

Investigators put additional pressure on Maggie by conducting multiple interviews with Dr. Ward even though they believed he had nothing additional to offer. Their strategy was effective in that the doctor regularly cautioned Maggie that she could be held criminally liable if she was intentionally protecting Bernard or misleading officials.

Despite their now substantial efforts, little progress was being made with their investigation. There was no sign of the elusive Bernard Patterson.

* * *

Eleven hundred miles away on the continent of Africa, Bernard was knowingly heading into the maelstrom. Characteristically, he was unafraid.

Reclaiming his Triumph 650 from a reluctant and disappointed Berber herdsman, Bernard wisely paid him a generous caretaker's fee. Otherwise, he probably wouldn't have gotten out of Ghadames alive. Feeling a sense of urgency, he hurriedly left the oasis and wheeled steadily north on a tiring, long day's journey to Tunis where he found a room. Recovering from his sojourn in the desert, he immediately bought new clothes, showered and meticulously groomed himself for a return to England and Maggie. Bernard gave the motorcycle to a hotel clerk as reward for finding him a hefty supply of wine and arranging for a prostitute to visit him in his room.

Taking a cab to Tunis-Carthage Airport, Bernard secured a ticket for the next flight to Heathrow in London. Realizing that he was soaring toward some serious potential problems, he spent much of his four-hour flight chain smoking cigarettes, drinking Beaujolais, and reminiscing about previous return trips to Vietnam. The perils he faced in the present paled by comparison with those he'd confronted back then. He would tough this out just as he had many more dangerous missions in the past.

Money was another looming problem. While he still had a modest supply remaining, he was running low on cash. What he would do when he ran out was unclear. Perhaps he and Maggie could move to Spain and work his half interest in the restaurant in Malaga. Calling her was the first thing on his agenda after he arrived in London.

For Bernard, selling pot had been a reliable source of income in Vietnam. Smuggling cheap Vietnamese pot home, it had been a big money maker for him during his short visits to Mars Hill between tours of duty in Vietnam. While stationed with the 101st Airborne Division near

Hue in 1969, in addition to fanatically hunting down the enemy, he had operated a flourishing marijuana business. Remembering the accidental meeting with his childhood buddy, Doug Pierce, his mind drifted back to Vietnam.

On leave at Camp Eagle on the coast of the South China Sea east of Hue, he was sitting in the shade of his hooch when Doug and another soldier walked by on their way to the beach. Yelling out his name, they relived memories of Mars Hill and their last visits home. Offering him pot, he was surprised to learn that Doug was a nonsmoker; there weren't many. Doug's companion quickly accepted the offer and Bernard later scored a substantial sale. In a few hours, Doug was gone. They didn't see each other again until he returned to Mars Hill after leaving the service. That often happened in Vietnam: people were quickly in and out of your life, sometimes forever.

Pot smoking had not been an option since he'd left the motorcycle gang in Bologna. Bernard missed it. Pot had a calming effect on him. Maggie had connections with the drug world in London. With her help, he'd find some. If he could locate a reliable source and negotiate a middleman arrangement, maybe he could get into selling again. Possibilities for earning money were always available for a resourceful entrepreneur.

While British authorities were determinably

searching for bank robber and fugitive Bernard Patterson, the prevailing assumption was that he was already somewhere in England. No one expected him to be returning to England, especially from Africa. United Kingdom Revenue and Customs was not on alert for that eventuality. Bernard encountered no difficulties passing through customs and entering the British Isles as Robert Inman.

Shortly after he arrived at Heathrow, he called Maggie. Terrified that she was being watched, Maggie refused to see him in Staines. Pressuring to meet her, she reluctantly agreed to join him in a hotel at the airport as driving there would probably not arouse suspicions, if the police were indeed spying on her. Her intuition was absolutely correct; they were. However, once it was apparent that Maggie was on her way to the airport, they discontinued surveillance.

The meeting between Bernard and Maggie was bittersweet. After intense lovemaking, Maggie made it clear that law enforcement officials suspected her of collusion and they couldn't continue seeing each other. Otherwise, he would most certainly be apprehended and she would be prosecuted as an accomplice. Even if he was willing to take the risk, she wasn't. However, she still recommended the Isle of Jersey as a possible safe haven. They reluctantly parted company.

After Maggie left, Bernard immediately hired

a cab for the trip to Portsmouth where he took the ferry back to the scenic Isle of Jersey. Quite disappointed that Maggie wouldn't accompany him, he was buoyed by positive memories of his past visit to the picturesque island that reminded him of the Maine coastline.

* * *

An essential element of their ongoing investigation, detectives from Scotland Yard attempted to interview all of Maggie's neighbors. During their first sweep, they missed Mary Porter, who had been away. She was home when investigators returned a second time.

A very observant neighbor, the seventy-one-year-old Porter remembered seeing a young man who fit Bernard Patterson's description frequenting Maggie's flat a few weeks prior. He regularly used her sports car and they were often together. On a couple of occasions, she had seen him with other women. Porter couldn't remember exactly when but at some point shortly before she stopped seeing him, another young man joined him briefly and they were both riding motorcycles. She only saw the other man a couple of times but she was able to provide a reasonably good description. Porter did not know any of his other female companions but was unimpressed with what she perceived as their loose moral behavior.

Again interviewing Maggie and Dr. Ward, neither of them had any knowledge of the motorcycles or the other man. Authorities were now searching for Bernard and a second man who were believed to be using motorcycles as their means of transportation. Where they had obtained them was also a new aspect of the investigation.

* * *

While traveling on the ferry to the Isle of Jersey, Bernard cultivated a friendship with two attractive youthful Irish ladies named Colleen and Shauna. Returning from a visit to their native Ireland, they were now going back to their home on the island. When they arrived at the ferry landing in St. Helier, the alluring women invited him to their fishing hut. That was an offer Bernard couldn't refuse.

Transplants from the old fishing village of Kilmore Quay in Ireland, the two lovely Irish ladies lived with Colleen's husband Dillon, who was Shauna's brother. They barely subsisted residing in a small rustic cabin in the coastal village of Gorey on the east side of the island. All three were intimately involved in the tight-knit local commercial fishing community. Dillon was trying to eke out a living selling his catch to island stores and the wealthy bluebloods who maintained seasonal homes on the island. Bernard was immediately and warmly welcomed, especially after he began buying food and drink for the comparatively poor fishing family.

A familiar pattern renewed. Just as he had in Mars Hill, California, Switzerland, and Italy, Bernard funded what became a perpetual party. However, this time he elevated his promiscuity to a new and dangerous level. Secretly carrying on torrid affairs with both Shauna and Colleen, the three of them sometimes slept together. Dillon, who was a mountain of a man and generally angry with the world, would not have approved.

* * *

Canvassing all motorcycle dealers in the Staines area, investigators found a retailer who had sold two Triumphs to a small, young American man who was accompanied by a Canadian friend. The purchaser had paid cash and their copy of the sales invoice indicated his name was Robert Inman. Impressed with him at the time, as he was an exceptionally unusual customer, the dealer recalled many of the details of the transaction—recollecting in particular that they had mentioned something about taking the ferry to France and riding in the Alps.

Scotland Yard promptly notified French and Swiss officials that they should be on the alert for the two motorcyclists while simultaneously dispatching detectives to the various ferry terminals in search of clues. A determination was also made to initiate another series of interrogations with Dr. Ward and his transparently evasive daughter.

* * *

Bernard and his newfound fishing playmates in Gorey were throwing the latest in an almost continuous succession of huge parties at the fishing hut. A loud raucous affair with excessive drinking and abundant pot, not only did it attract the attention of the hard-drinking local fishermen, but agitated many of the nearby upscale neighbors. After several complaints were lodged by influential citizens, police raided the party.

When authorities arrived, they demanded identification from all participants. Concerned about his fraudulent documentation, Bernard, who admitted to being an American, falsely claimed that he was Jack Scott and had misplaced his passport. Suspicious, they gave him forty-eight hours to present evidence of his identity at police headquarters. Despite a large crowd of volatile intoxicated fishermen, the party was disbanded without further problems or any arrests.

Law enforcement officials also sent a routine message to Scotland Yard informing them that they had encountered an American named Jack Scott who could not provide his passport or proof of his identity. Their guidance was requested.

After developing boat engine problems while fishing the following day, a frustrated, discouraged Dillon returned to his hut prematurely. He found Bernard in bed with his wife and sister. Enraged at what he considered to be the ultimate insult by a guest in his house, the huge fisherman thrashed Bernard and both women badly. Fortunate to escape with his life, Bernard quickly vacated the premises.

* * *

Dr. Ward had been concealing one piece of information from authorities. The deliberate omission hadn't been to protect Maggie, rather his pride. Relatives had previously informed him of their meeting with Maggie and her American boyfriend at the family home in St. Helier. Apprehensive about getting them involved in the sordid affair, he had remained silent on the matter. When detectives from Scotland Yard recontacted him, the aristocratic doctor finally relented, relating that Maggie may have traveled to the Isle of Jersey with Patterson in April.

Maggie broke down and confessed when confronted with the latest revelation, admitting that she had intentionally avoided mentioning their visit to St. Helier. Under further intense questioning, she also disclosed that she had recently met him at a hotel in Heathrow. Although she didn't know his current whereabouts, she speculated that he may have returned to the Isle of Jersey. Maggie was charged with obstruction of justice.

* * *

Seriously beaten, concerned about his scheduled meeting with local police, low on money, and having no place to go, Bernard decided to take the ferry back to Portsmouth. When he arrived, he'd find a way to contact Maggie.

• 20 •

Rat Trap

*"I don't think it could have been done
any other way. At least I did it."*
—Bernard Patterson

Scotland Yard had no files or information on an American named Jack Scott. When they received the police report from the Isle of Jersey regarding his lack of a passport, there was no significant cause for concern. However, detectives assigned the Bernard Patterson/Robert Inman case were actively exploring all possible avenues of inquiry. As a result of their most recent interrogation of Maggie Ward, they were particularly interested in anything unusual or suspect involving the Isle of Jersey. When one of the investigators read the Scott report, he was quick to speculate on a possible connection.

Police officials on the Isle of Jersey were immediately contacted. The description of Patterson fit that of Jack Scott, who was due to report to the police station the first thing the following morning with proof of his identity.

Scotland Yard advised that there was a distinct possibility that Scott was actually Bernard Patterson, an American bank robber, and directed that if located he should be detained until agents arrived. Since a handgun had been used in the robbery and he was believed to be a decorated Vietnam combat veteran, they cautioned that Patterson should be considered dangerous.

The alleged Jack Scott did not report as directed. Authorities in Scotland Yard and on the Isle of Jersey mobilized, now theorizing that he was quite probably Bernard Patterson.

Without further delay, Scotland Yard sent two agents in an aerial unit aircraft on a cross-channel flight to the Jersey Airport. They would arrive at the airport in the parish of Saint Peter five miles northwest of Saint Helier later in the day. A manhunt for Bernard Patterson had commenced. It was Friday, June 9, 1972.

* * *

After spending the night in a motel in Saint Helier recovering from the brawl with Dillon, Bernard took a cab directly to the ferry terminal. The next ferry to Portsmouth was scheduled to depart at 4:20 that afternoon. Concerned that he might be recognized by police, Bernard resolved to wait as inconspicuously as possible in the terminal for the remainder of the day.

* * *

Since the now suspected bank robber Jack Scott had not appeared for his scheduled interview, two Isle of Jersey police officers were dispatched to the fisherman's cabin in Gorey. When they arrived furnishings were found strewn about the hut in disarray and the household was in obvious turmoil. After a marathon drinking bout, Dillon had passed out on the kitchen floor. Both visibly battered, Colleen and Shauna were packing their bags, planning a return to Ireland.

The beleaguered women declined to implicate Dillon as the cause of their injuries, stating they had both fallen onto the deck of Dillon's fishing vessel during rough seas. Doubting their explanation but primarily concerned with finding someone purporting to be Jack Scott, they inquired on his whereabouts. Relating that Scott had left the previous day, the women had no idea where he had gone and when or if he would return. Frightened and very wary of the police, they were evasive in answering questions about Scott who they knew as Robert Inman, a fact they didn't share. Neither of them had ever heard of anyone named Bernard Patterson.

Too groggy and inebriated to coherently communicate, attempts to question Dillon failed. Since their primary mission was to locate and detain Scott as quickly as possible, the officers didn't have time to sober up Dillon or investigate a possible domestic dispute. They left to make further inquiries with neighbors. No one in the area had any information of value but virtually everyone agreed that if Scott or Patterson was the person responsible for all of the raucous parties, they hoped he was gone permanently.

* * *

Sitting in the ferry terminal lobby, Bernard contemplated his immediate future. Prospects were grim. The major advantage he'd had since leaving Mars Hill was money. Now it was almost gone. His only reliable connection in England was Maggie who was being watched by police and would likely be resistant to seeing him. Still, he had been in much worse predicaments and endured, sometimes prospered.

The ability to blend into a situation or circumstance and become unnoticed, almost invisible had been one of the truly exceptional traits that helped Bernard survive and excel in Vietnam. Remaining completely silent and essentially indistinguishable while observing everything around him, even the smallest details had facilitated his escape from many harrowing situations in the tunnels and jungles. That talent had been utilized again hiding out after the robbery. Now, he needed to call on this unique skill once more.

After landing at the airport, the two Scotland Yard detectives met with Isle of Jersey police officials a little after 1 o'clock. Since the suspect had not appeared as required and could not be located, the collective assumption was that he had left or was attempting to leave the island.

Typical of many island communities, the ferry terminal in Saint Helier was a hub of activity and the primary means of entering and leaving the island. While law enforcement officials throughout the island had been placed on alert, the focal point of their investigation would be the terminal. Contacting the ferry business office by telephone, they confirmed that Robert Inman had made reservations for the 4:20 departure to Portsmouth. His current location was unknown.

Formulating a plan to unobtrusively search the facility, teams of island law enforcement officials would be placed at all points of egress. The two Scotland Yard agents accompanied by local officers who had questioned Bernard at the party and could recognize him would scour the interior in street clothes. Clearly outnumbering and presumably outgunning him, the primary concern was public safety if he was located and resisted arrest in the busy terminal. Assuming that he was there, they intended to quietly tighten the net around him.

Having impatiently sat for several hours smoking cigarettes and drinking coffee, the time was 3:30 p.m. and the ferry would be loading soon. Bernard left his seat to use the toilet before boarding. Stepping out of the restroom after finishing, he walked directly into the path of the completely astonished law enforcement contingent.

Instantly recognizing him, they surrounded and instructed Bernard to halt and raise his hands. Accepting that the game was up and devoid of options, Bernard did not resist. When questioned, he freely admitted being the infamous American bank robber, Bernard Patterson. He was carrying a passport for Robert Peter Inman.

Bernard possessed 5,000 Swiss francs or $1,315 in American money when apprehended. That was all that remained of the stolen cash he had brought with him when leaving California. A major concentration of the follow-up investigation would be what happened to the missing money.

When he entered Europe in December, Bernard was carrying $90,000 American money that would approximate $700,000 in present-day value. The exchange rate in Switzerland was about four to one at the time and generally greater depending upon the country he was in. A reasonable approximation would be that he squandered the equivalent of $1.5 or $2 million by current standards while living the high life during in his seven-month madcap escapade. He had almost fulfilled his stated goal of spending everything before getting caught.

After traveling almost 20,000 miles through seven countries on three continents by airplane, automobile, boat, and motorcycle in just a little under seven months, Bernard's remarkable, improbable journey as a much sought after fugitive bank robber was over. Obviously embarrassed, law enforcement officials on two continents had difficulty believing that an unsophisticated, undereducated young man from rural northern Maine could have accomplished all that he had while successfully eluding highly trained investigators from several countries. They were actively considering alternative explanations or conspiracy theories.

While Bernard experienced more than his share of good fortune, he was also badly underestimated. The innate skills he possessed that had been honed and perfected in Vietnam substantially benefited him while on the lam. He was extremely intelligent and very calculating. Most important, Bernard was fearless enough to do the unexpected with a brazen confidence that defied predictability.

In the world according to Bernard, he had been a huge success. In his words, "There was no sense fooling myself into thinking that I could make it into a fortune or something like that. I knew what most of it was all about. It was a high, a great high for a while, but then I crashed. I don't think it could have been done any other way. At least I did it."

Now he was going to pay a very steep price for his extended high.

• 21 •

Show Me the Money

"The rest (of the money) *is just gone,*
spent . . . that is all I know about the crime."
—Attorney Paul Zendzian

The FBI was notified by Scotland Yard of the
capture of Bernard Patterson who had been
using the passport of Robert Inman and had
also assumed the alias of Jack Scott. Proceedings
were initiated for his extradition back to the
United States.

Bernard would have plenty of time to reminisce
about his past adventures while contemplating
his future. Confined to Pentonville Prison in
North London, he languished there for a long,
monotonous summer while extradition negotiations were conducted. A dreary 130-year-old
facility located in the London Borough of
Islington, it had formerly been the site of
numerous executions by hanging, the most
recent one being a young man about Bernard's
age just eleven years earlier. In the not too
distant past, that might have been Bernard's
fate.

During his stay in Pentonville, Bernard initiated several attempts to contact Maggie. She never responded.

* * *

When federal and local officials in Maine were notified that Bernard had been captured using the passport of Robert Inman, doubt and confusion regarding the true identity of the suspect detained in England and who they had imprisoned in Maine renewed. Questions arose as to why Patterson had been using the credentials of Robert Inman who was being held for murder in the Penobscot County Jail in Bangor or if the prisoner they had incarcerated was actually Robert Inman.

After further research, Assistant United States Attorney Kevin Cuddy disclosed that Patterson had assumed the identity of a Robert Inman from California and to the best of his knowledge had no relationship to the Inman being held in Bangor. Uncertainty, at least on the part of some, would continue to linger and be the cause of further conjecture until Bernard was returned to the United States.

* * *

After nearly three months of incarceration in Pentonville Prison, the Bow Street Court in London ordered Bernard's extradition to the United States on September 5, 1972. He had fifteen days to appeal. Ready to return home and escape his gloomy, isolated circumstances, no appellate action was commenced. Bernard had quickly learned that prison life did not agree with his energetic, peripatetic personality.

Two United States Marshals were sent to London to escort Bernard back. Coincidentally, the officer in charge was Deputy U.S. Marshal Guy Patterson of Clinton, Maine. They were not related. On the return flight, Bernard and his namesake developed a rapport engaging in a very animated almost nonstop conversation. Guy Patterson would later recount that Bernard was a very interesting character and "nobody's fool."

They arrived back in the United States on Monday night, October 9, 1972. The following day, Bernard was brought before the U.S. Magistrate for the Eastern District of New York in Brooklyn for a bail hearing. Assuming that he had hidden some or all of the stolen money, the magistrate determined that $100,000, the approximate amount of cash he had allegedly absconded with in the robbery, was the appropriate bail.

Unable to post bail, Bernard was remanded to the U.S. District Court of Maine charged with bank robbery and commission of a felony with a firearm. After a short flight to Maine, he appeared before U.S. Magistrate Brian Keith in Bangor on Tuesday, October 17. Magistrate

Keith determined that he was unable to hire an attorney and appointed Paul Zendzian of Bangor to represent him. A plea of innocent was entered. While awaiting trial, Bernard was to be held in the Penobscot County Jail in Bangor, the same location as that of murderer Robert Inman.

Bernard was also wanted for the August 14, 1971, burglary of Al's Diner in Mars Hill and additional crimes related to the bank robbery under State of Maine law. Aroostook County District Attorney Cecil Burleigh indicated that further prosecutions would be forthcoming once the federal issues were resolved.

* * *

What happened to the money was a major concern for the court, law enforcement officials, and the bonding company that had covered the bank's loss. U.S. Attorney Peter Mills announced that at the time of his arrest Patterson had only the equivalent of $1,315 on his person. Mills had no information on any remaining money and as far as he knew, none had been found.

On the advice of his attorney, Bernard initially declined to answer any questions posed by investigators regarding the robbery, his activities during the past year, or the location of any remaining stolen money. Rumors were rampant that he had hidden a large sum of money in Maine. During an exercise break at the jail, two inmates tried to beat the information out of him. Bernard was placed in isolation for his protection.

After further deliberations with his counsel Paul Zendzian, Bernard decided to change his plea and cooperate with law enforcement. During a meeting with officials, he provided them with specific information on how he had concealed $17,000 in a coffee can near Mars Hill Mountain Road. Accompanied by officers of the court, Bernard led them directly to the location and the money was recovered. However, over $90,000 could not be accounted for, and the best information Bernard could provide was that he'd spent it while on the run in Europe.

* * *

On November 20, 1972, court officials made public that suspected Mars Hill bank robber Bernard Patterson had agreed to change his innocent plea. A hearing was scheduled for the U.S. District Court in Bangor on December 5.

Described by reporters as a good-looking, dapper, mustachioed young man wearing a well-tailored suit and stylish boots, Bernard was escorted to U.S. District Court by Deputy U.S. Marshals Charles Pooler and Robert Crabb on Tuesday, December 5, 1972. Venerable, prominent federal Judge Edward T. Gignoux was presiding.

When asked for his plea by Judge Gignoux, Bernard's defense attorney Paul Zendzian announced that Bernard wished to plead nolo contendere, meaning he did not want to contest the charges but there was no explicit admission of guilt. His attorney postulated that since there were additional Aroostook County indictments filed against Bernard concerning the bank robbery and Al's Diner burglary, a guilty plea could be used against him in those cases.

Zendzian further stated, "As to the best of his ability, Mr. Patterson recognizes what the law is and wishes to protect himself."

While Judge Gignoux acknowledged that a 1959 U.S. Supreme Court ruling might allow for the prosecution of Bernard on state charges without constituting double jeopardy, he declined to accept the nolo contendere plea. Stating that he was not prepared to impose a sentence based on such a plea, the judge emphasized that he required a formal admission by Bernard that he had committed the crime before issuing his determination. Or he could continue with his innocent plea and a trial date would be scheduled.

During a protracted consultation with his attorney, they discussed the potential negative impact of pursuing an innocent plea given the overwhelming evidence against him. Believing it to be a futile effort that would only act to frustrate the court, possibly resulting in a harsher sentence, Bernard entered a plea of guilty.

U.S. Attorney Peter Mills testified that there was substantial evidence of Patterson's guilt that justified the maximum prison sentence provided by law. Noting that Bernard had recently traveled to Mars Hill under the custody of FBI agents and federal marshals where he had led them to $17,000 that he admitted having concealed after the bank robbery. The remaining $90,000 was still missing and Patterson had conceded to agents that he had spent or given it away. Further, testimony would show that after escaping to California, he had purchased the passport of a Robert Peter Inman for $400 with the intent of fleeing to Europe.

Mills also related that while Patterson was in Europe, he had divulged robbing the Northern National Bank during phone conversations with Aroostook County Deputy Sheriff Edgar Wheeler and his former girlfriend. Finally, when apprehended by Scotland Yard detectives on the Isle of Jersey, he had readily confessed to the crime.

Bernard took the stand providing brief testimony in which he openly admitted committing the robbery. In a low, hushed voice, he meticulously detailed how he had "pulled off" the crime and escaped, emphasizing that he had used an unloaded twenty-two caliber pistol.

Attorney Paul Zendzian presented mitigating factors that he asserted merited a light sentence with an emphasis on rehabilitation. Focusing on Bernard's exceptional military record, he detailed the numerous medals he had received for heroic action as a tunnel rat and paratrooper during multiple tours of duty in Vietnam. As an example of his meritorious service, he related an incident when Bernard had courageously taken command of his platoon in combat. Not only had he fought bravely but there were many instances where he had assumed responsibility for the safety of his fellow soldiers, saving several lives.

Referring to his military record, Zendzian observed, "A man who has done all of this is hard to understand when it comes to committing a crime." When responding to Judge Gignoux's questions about what motivated Bernard to do it and what caused the breakdown in character, he responded, "I don't believe he knows himself."

His counsel also pointed out that Bernard had cooperated with law enforcement officials and that had resulted in recovery of $17,000. The fact that the bank robbery was the largest in State of Maine history was purely coincidental, he reflected. Bernard had only expected to get a few thousand dollars.

In summation, Zendzian further opined that Bernard was a man of character and that when coupled with his distinguished combat service he was a very good candidate for rehabilitation. A long, harsh prison sentence would simply be inappropriate in his situation.

U.S. Attorney Mills countered by emphasizing the magnitude of the crime and the need to deter others. Given these factors, he strongly advocated that a long prison sentence was warranted.

Judge Gignoux took time to concentrate on what happened to the money. Addressing Bernard, he stated, "I find it quite incredible that you could have disposed of that amount of money in about six months." The judge wondered aloud whether there was still money remaining. Zendzian responded that the "rest of the money to the best of my knowledge was used in Europe."

"You say, you . . . $93,000 you spent over in Europe in six months," Gignoux inquired. "What about verification of this?" he wanted to know.

"He's not indicated to me any names of individuals," his attorney admitted. "He has told me there is none. I don't believe there is. The rest is just gone, spent . . . that is all I know about the crime."

A World War II veteran himself, Judge Gignoux

was obviously somewhat sympathetic with Bernard. Feeling that his military service should factor into the sentence, Gignoux observed that the country owed him a "real debt." Concluding, however, that his service did not give him the prerogative to return from the war and commit serious, self-serving crimes. To accept such a premise was an invitation to anarchy, he observed.

After further deliberation, Judge Gignoux discerned that there had been a wave of bank robberies and airline hijackings throughout the country in recent years, several involving returning Vietnam veterans. He deemed that when all factors were considered, a substantial prison sentence was warranted. Judge Gignoux sentenced Bernard to serve fifteen years for the first count of bank robbery and ten years on the second count for use of a firearm during commission of the crime. He was to be transferred to the federal prison facility in Lewisburg in central Pennsylvania to serve out his time. Observers stated that Bernard was characteristically cool when he received the sentence.

While this was a tougher sentence than desired, Judge Gignoux had actually been quite considerate in his decision as the maximum sentence for the two crimes was thirty years if served consecutively. However, since he determined that the two counts should be completed concurrently, the effective sentence was fifteen years.

More important for Bernard was an additional stipulation that Judge Gignoux included. Acknowledging his military service and the significant potential for rehabilitation, the judge instructed the Board of Parole to release him at "any time" they deemed appropriate. That opened the door for a much shorter period of imprisonment.

The first six months of incarceration had been almost unbearable for Bernard. Now he was faced with confinement for an indeterminate period in the Lewisburg Federal penitentiary, home to some of the country's most notorious criminals.

• 22 •

Scared Rat

*"Of all the things I did in Vietnam,
I was never more afraid than in prison."*
—Bernard Patterson

Located in the tranquil farmlands of central Pennsylvania, outwardly Lewisburg Federal Penitentiary seemed a reasonably harmonious place. The appearance was deceptive. Housing some of the most disreputable, dangerous criminals of that era, it was often perilous and unforgiving.

Al Capone, John Gotti, and Whitey Bulger had passed through its cell doors, and Jimmy Hoffa was released the year before Bernard arrived. Almost mirroring Bernard's time at Lewisburg, the infamous Henry Hill of the Lucchese crime family was an inmate from 1972 to 1978. Although he was suspected of committing a plethora of heinous crimes throughout his entire adult life, including a $400,000 Air France robbery, Hill was incarcerated for the relatively minor conviction of extortion. The obvious benefits of having an exceptional defense team had not been available to war hero Bernard Patterson. Ray Liotta would later portray Hill in the movie *Goodfellas.*

During the period that Bernard was imprisoned, Lewisburg housed an unusually large population of organized crime members. Among them were Paul Dario, Jimmy Doyle, some of his gang, and several members of the Gotti family. The notorious Johnny Dio, convicted for the acid blinding of newspaper columnist Victor Riesal and several sharp shooters from the East Harlem Purple Gang were part of the institution's ruthless clientele. Confining over one thousand inmates in the sprawling facility, it was inundated with prisoners associated with the mob. Lewisburg was a veritable who's who of organized crime.

Having access to large sums of money to bribe corrupt officials and guards, mobsters dominated the prison, which also included the usual assortment of murderers, rapists, sociopaths, and psychopaths. Extremely unpleasant things happened to anyone who challenged them or their authority.

Bernard's new home was a very unsavory place.

* * *

Prior to his arrival at Lewisburg Penitentiary in December 1972, Bernard's experiences in Pentonville Prison and the Penobscot County

Jail had been comparatively benign. Normally isolated from the worst of the prison population, with the exception of the one Penobscot County Jail beating, his previous jail time had been essentially incident free. Lewisburg would prove to be a very different, extremely dangerous intimidating environment for Bernard.

A small, handsome, fit young man; within hours of his arrival other inmates were competing to determine who would be fortunate enough to claim Bernard as their new "bitch." Although an exceptionally tough, hardened combat veteran, he was no match for many of the much larger, stronger convicts who were vying for the latest boy toy. Lacking his forty-five caliber pistol, M-16, or bayonet to level the playing field, Bernard was at a substantial disadvantage. Unlike the jungles or tunnels of Vietnam, there were no obvious places for him to blend in or conceal himself.

Gangs permeated the prison culture and mobster gangs were the ruling class within the confines of the Lewisburg prison walls. While gangs were the source of a multitude of problems in the facility, they provided members with one very significant benefit, protection. Anyone who didn't join or wasn't accepted into a gang was exposed to the worst of an unmerciful subterranean society. Bernard was not a joiner.

What status Bernard would achieve in this perverse institutional pecking order had yet to be determined. The first test in the almost ritualistic process was finding out how tough he really was or if his leathery outer demeanor was a cover for weakness. Experienced cons knew how to recognize the difference. There was no shortage of predators looking for vulnerable victims or sadists anxious to abuse the latest arrival for fun and pleasure.

Bernard would later relate to a friend, "Of all the things I did in Vietnam, I was never more afraid than in prison." Believing that he'd been marked by the prison gangs, Bernard constantly feared he'd get a "knife in his back." Anxious about the possibility of gang rape or worse, he was afraid to walk the halls by himself and "never wanted to be alone in the shower." A consummate warrior in combat, these ominous forebodings never diminished during his entire stay in Lewisburg.

Complicating his dubious situation, rumors circulated that he still had some of the stolen money hidden somewhere, probably in Maine or California. Destitute convicts nearing their release or those having connections on the outside had a special interest in getting to know Bernard.

Early on, Bernard was challenged to a fight by one of the bigger, tougher inmates in his cell block. Instinctively taking the offensive, he preemptively inflicted serious pain on his adversary with a powerful blow to his temple, dazing him. After that, Bernard got the worst of it as his much larger aggressor dominated the brawl. The other convicts warily ignored the entire incident. Even though he lost the fight, Bernard earned grudging respect from his attacker and the prison community. This event more than any other brought him to the realization that he needed to utilize all of his native intelligence and survival skills if he was to avoid being a victim of the most degrading, perverse aspects of the brutal prison culture.

Many of the lessons he'd learned in Vietnam were now of substantial benefit to Bernard. Recognizing that prison life had a multitude of similarities to a war zone, he committed himself to finding ways to survive just as he had in Vietnam. Analogous to fighting the Viet Cong, he must never be indecisive or exhibit weakness. Predators always attacked the most vulnerable first. Life experience had taught him how to deal with bullies—send a not so subtle message that they would pay a serious price for screwing with him. While not looking for a fight, he would quickly strike out if challenged.

A little guy, the alternative to perpetual vigilance and preemptive action was life as a prison bitch. Someone who would be a plaything passed from one deranged predator to another. Not only was that a role completely foreign and offensive to Bernard, but a circumstance that was ultimately much more insecure than fighting back. Bitches inevitably ended up victims of the most sadistic, violent psychopaths in the system.

Nights were the worst. The intense loneliness reminded him of when he'd been lost in the Sahara Desert, except at least he'd had freedom of movement in the desert. Ruefully yearning for his independence, friends and particularly female companionship and affection, Bernard wanted out. More than anything, night and day, during every waking moment, he desperately wanted out. At night, alone in his cell he reflected on his dire situation. Despair was an insidious, nightly adversary.

Like crawling in the tunnels, Bernard needed to be hypervigilant, always listening and observing what was happening around him. Warily interacting with the other inmates, he learned to share nothing about himself and inquire very cautiously of others. A compulsive gambler, Bernard avoided all games of chance. Broke, he couldn't repay gambling debts if he lost. Unpaid debts were an invitation for retaliation. Never rat on a fellow inmate was a lesson quickly learned. That guaranteed violent retribution.

Concluding that getting out as soon as possible was his best chance for staying alive, he initiated a strategy to attain that goal. Always on his best behavior, Bernard respected the prison staff without kissing up or brown nosing. Working out regularly to stay fit and better protect himself, he otherwise found the library was the best and safest place to pass the time. Bernard became a regular at the library.

Although he only had a ninth-grade education, Bernard was a virtual math whiz. A skill he had sharpened to near perfection trading various currencies in the Vietnamese black market, Bernard instinctively understood mathematics and could explain it to others. He had the unique capacity to see numbers in his mind and could visualize complex mathematical transactions. Using all of his wits, Bernard negotiated an assignment to the prison library where he obtained a position as a math instructor teaching other inmates. Through his use of guile, brazen confidence, and innate ability, he managed to get himself separated from the worst of the prison environment and into a relatively safe situation. A ninth-grade dropout was now teaching high school level math courses to the prison population.

Like the Glacier des Bossons he had visited in Chamonix, time began to pass ever so gradually.

* * *

In the summer of 1973, Bernard's attorney, Paul Zendzian, contacted him with an interesting proposition. A writer named Ronald Bean wanted to interview him about his experiences as a bank robber and while on the run in California and Europe. Bean would be collaborating with *Bangor Daily News* staff writer John Day. Zendzian strongly recommended he consent to meet with Bean.

Bernard didn't need prompting. Any escape from the monotony of prison life was in itself an engaging possibility. The prospect of telling his story to others appealed to his ego. It would also provide the opportunity to publicly refute the widely held misconception that there was still money hidden, an ongoing source of problems for him. Bernard readily agreed.

The result of their meetings was a series of three newspaper articles in October 1973. For the first time readers, and his friends and family, learned the full magnitude of his colossal adventure. From that point on, an almost legendary, mythical persona was attributed to Bernard by many. That was a role he enthusiastically embraced.

The articles also precipitated several book and movie proposals. Despite being penniless, Bernard would have nothing to do with selling himself cheap. Stubbornly demanding serious up-front money, none of the schemes ever came to fruition.

Instead, Bernard had another idea for earning his fortune after being released.

* * *

Working in the library had an ancillary benefit for Bernard. It afforded him the opportunity to study botany. Convinced that the sale of marijuana could be a profit-making venture for him after his parole from prison, Bernard researched the subject with a vengeance. The result was that he acquired a cogent scientific knowledge of Cannabis and the techniques necessary to grow healthy marijuana-producing plants with the highest possible concentration of THC, the chemical that provides the hallucinogenic effects from smoking pot.

Learning how to develop the most potent strains without wasting years on experimentation like many novice growers helped prepare him for his new career. Uniquely important to Bernard, he educated himself on methods of harvesting pot where there was a short growing season, such as northern Maine. Identifying varieties that had the best potential for early maturation was one of the significant benefits of his investigations.

Bernard's research indicated that the ideal habitat for safe and efficient growth of the illegal substance was near riverbanks, meadows, and lands used for agriculture. Concealing the plants in an agricultural or forested environment provided the best overall protection from detection. He needed a location offering decent sunlight with an ample water supply and good drainage. Bernard knew some rural settings near Mars Hill that would meet that criterion. Once out of prison, farming was definitely in his future.

* * *

The years passed as Bernard studied botany, taught mathematics, took academic courses, and worked out while managing to avoid the worst aspects of the prison environment and its unsavory population. Remaining true to his strategic goal to obtain the earliest possible release, he was always on his best behavior and cooperative with prison officials. An excellent student and dedicated instructor, Bernard was a model prisoner. No one knew that he also excelled in the study of marijuana botany. Bernard's rehabilitation was nearly complete.

Besides botany, Bernard used his library time to do extensive research into psychological disorders. In the summer of 1976, he faked a nervous breakdown and was sent to the prison infirmary. For fifty-five days, medical experts treated and evaluated him. Although trained to identify imposters, they never detected that his illness was feigned. The consummate conman when he needed to be, Bernard was also a very good actor.

After he was discharged from the infirmary, Bernard used the fraudulent nervous breakdown as an argument to convince the Parole Board that he should be released early. Observing that as a result of this episode, he now realized that he'd been having severe psychological problems at the time he committed the robbery. Speculating that these issues were related to his combat experience, he suggested that not only did they explain his behavior at the time but that he now had the knowledge and skills to avoid such problems in the future.

Coupled with his exemplary behavior, the Board was persuaded. In early 1977, he was transferred to the Portland Halfway House with the opportunity for parole in six months.

Once at the halfway house, Bernard was determined to do whatever was necessary to ensure that he never returned to Lewisburg. While actively participating in all of the various programs offered to facilitate transition and reintegration into society, he met a counselor named Ruthanne.

A polished, well-educated woman, Ruthanne was energetic, focused, and committed to her work. Bernard was immediately impressed. They developed a strong mutual attraction that soon led to serious romance.

Fulfilling his commitment in the halfway house, they married. Bernard and his new wife returned to the Mars Hill area in the summer of 1977. Still recovering from his prison ordeal, Lewisburg had humbled him like no other life experience. Desirous of avoiding any undue fanfare or attention, Bernard insisted on maintaining a low profile while assimilating back into his former community where he had robbed the local bank.

On October 11, 1977, Bernard and Ruthanne acquired property from Ivan Upton in the Town of Westfield, a few miles north of Mars Hill. Since they didn't have the money to buy it, Upton took back a mortgage.

Ruthanne was soon able to obtain a position as an English professor at the University of Maine at Presque Isle. Resistant to the idea of working for someone else, instead of seeking employment and working a nine-to-five job, Bernard decided to fulfill his longtime dream. He would be a self-employed farmer.

Situated on the Young Lake Road in a very rural, remote setting, the real estate they were purchasing consisted of a small, ramshackle cabin and several acres of forest and farm land. With no close neighbors, it was the ideal location for Bernard to begin his new vocation as a pot farmer.

• 23 •

Living the High Life

"He was a real botanist. He learned to grow these two foot plants that no one could find . . . everyone knew he was growing pot but no one could find his plants."
—A friend

"Come out and visit sometime. The only people who visit me are the FBI and DEA."
—Bernard Patterson

Prison hadn't been good to Bernard. Despite earnest attempts to remain fit during his incarceration, friends were shocked with his appearance when he returned. At the young age of thirty, he looked old and gaunt.

Irrespective of his diminished demeanor, he still had a hunger for life and excitement. Soon after his return, Bernard was stopped for speeding on a motorcycle by his friend Deputy Sheriff Edgar Wheeler. Although only giving him a warning, this would be the beginning of decades of vehicular violations that included operating under the influence of alcohol, driving after license suspension, and speeding. He loved speed.

Normally, Bernard had friends chauffeur him. That was always a good decision because when he got behind the wheel of a car or on a motorcycle, there was almost always trouble. His license to drive was suspended much of the remainder of his life.

* * *

In the spring of 1978, Bernard began growing pot. Collaborating with a friend named Max, who already had a flourishing marijuana business a few miles away near the Canadian border, they combined Bernard's scientific knowledge with the hands-on experience Max had acquired to quickly grow and distribute a quality product that Bernard referred to as his "cash crop."

When his friend Kyle visited during the summer of 1978, Bernard already had a substantial, thriving array of plants spread over a wide expanse of land. Many were located on the property of abutting land owners. Touring the property with Bernard and Max, he was impressed with the two-foot dwarf plants that retained much of their potency but were extremely difficult to detect. Also cultivating an exceptional vegetable garden, his good friend departed Westfield believing Bernard was a remarkable botanist but also concerned with his heavy drinking.

Lacking the generous supply of cash Northern National Bank had unwillingly provided him while on the lam in Europe, Bernard's choice of alcoholic beverage had devolved. Instead of expensive wines and vintage Champagnes, he now drank cheap beer. When pot receipts were at their peak, he splurged on Budweiser and Miller High Life. Otherwise, he consumed the most inexpensive beer he could find. Brands such as Dawson, Narragansett, and Topper were frequently found in his fridge, although they didn't last long.

Later that summer, his longtime friend and army buddy Doug Pierce returned from Colorado in a truck camper. He found the chain smoking Bernard living a very unostentatious lifestyle in a tiny, primitive cabin. With the roof and windows being the only good things about the dilapidated structure, the hut barely qualified as adequate shelter. Bernard gave him the option of building a small place of his own on the land but he never did.

Doug camped on the property for a prolonged period. A party animal, Bernard regularly threw large bonfire celebrations that lasted deep into the night. Besides marathon bouts of drinking, copious amounts of pot were regularly provided.

Ever enigmatic, Bernard would at once be an active participant only to disappear then mysteriously reappear an hour or so later. Although Bernard didn't have a regular job, Doug observed that he always seemed to have money.

* * *

Mark Carney encountered Bernard again in 1978 while attending the University of Maine at Presque Isle where Ruthanne was his writing instructor. He first learned they were married when Bernard arrived at the campus to pick her up. Although friends since high school, their relationship had become somewhat strained and awkward as Mark couldn't reconcile that Bernard had burglarized his uncle, owner of Al's Diner. However, they did have conversations about his experiences in prison and life as a fugitive in Europe. Like others, Carney was surprised to see how much he seemed to have aged in prison. Haggard beyond his years, youth had prematurely departed. He also couldn't help but notice that Bernard rarely made eye contact, rather his eyes seemed to dart suspiciously about.

Mark and Ruthanne were also friends. Relating that she had fallen in love with Bernard while working at the halfway house, she now found him difficult to live with. Recognizing that he was incredibly intelligent with a lot of depth to his personality, Ruthanne struggled to under-stand him. He had erected an impenetrable wall around himself that couldn't be pierced.

Life was much less than idyllic for Ruthanne and Bernard in their remote Westfield cabin. Although they soon had a daughter, the marriage didn't last.

* * *

While other aspects of his life were imperfect, the pot business was prospering. Averaging $30,000 to $40,000 a year in sales, Bernard had a good income that was sufficient to sustain the lifestyle he had chosen despite his spend-thrift inclinations when money was plentiful. Because his pot receipts were tied to the growing season, he would earn most of his income after the crop was harvested in the fall and start running low on cash by the following summer. The sporadic nature of his income sometimes resulted in a feast or famine existence but there was never a shortage of pot. Occasionally, he supplemented his marijuana earnings with legal employment doing construc-tion or work related to the potato farming industry.

When Bernard did find outside employment, he had the reputation of being an extremely hard worker. While the Canadian border crossing in nearby Houlton was being built, he worked as a mason tender. Normally one tender was assigned to each mason. The heavy smoking

Bernard incredibly tended three masons without missing an assignment.

On at least one occasion, lawful work morphed into the realm of the illicit. Hired to operate a fertilizer plant, Bernard oversaw filling storage tanks with about forty tons of fertilizer. A few days later, he reported to his supervisor that the tanks were mysteriously empty. About $10,000 in product had inexplicably disappeared. Assigned the task of carefully watching the property for a possible return of the thieves, after a week of monitoring Bernard disclosed that no one had materialized.

Concluding that it must have been an inside job, his manager threatened to contact the police. Fearing a return to prison, Bernard confessed to the crime and an earlier instance when he had traded four tons of fertilizer for some beef cattle. Considering him a friend and not wanting to be responsible for his incarceration, his supervisor decided not to pursue prosecution and restitution was informally arranged with Bernard's collaborator, who had trucked the fertilizer away to his farm. Despite his subsequent firing, the two remained friends and Bernard often stopped by his house to visit, one time bringing his newborn baby daughter.

Rumors began to circulate that he had a lucrative marijuana business. That news inevitably found its way to the law enforcement community. The National Guard began conducting a surveillance of the vicinity during the late summer of 1982. Using low-flying helicopters, they carefully scrutinized the entire area without success. Failing that, the Guard established a bivouac in nearby E Plantation with the intent of conducting a more thorough boots on the ground investigation.

A close friend of Bernard was a member of the Guard unit and tipped him off that a massive, clandestine nighttime search was planned for the immediate future. Bernard harvested the entire crop prior to their arrival and concealed it with Max in a hidden storage location just across the border in New Brunswick, Canada.

Scores of soldiers from the National Guard spent countless man hours scouring Bernard's land. When they arrived at his hut the following morning, he was nonchalantly sitting out front with a can of Budweiser in hand and a sardonic smile on his face. No trace was found of any marijuana plants or other evidence of illegal activities despite an exhaustive search. Several members of the unit were some of his regular marijuana customers.

Later, Bernard had a conversation with Duane Grass, Mars Hill fireman and potato farmer, who also operated a small trucking business. Proposing that Duane transport a load of organic wheat to central Maine, he declined. That was probably a very judicious decision.

* * *

In the summer of 1988, Kyle returned. Amazed with the sophisticated nature and scale of the pot operation, he stayed on for an extended period. During their weeks of smoking pot, drinking cheap beer, and reminiscing, Bernard shared many stories.

An inveterate storyteller with a wealth of entertaining experiences, Bernard had an abundance of tales to relate. While Vietnam was often the focus, two of the more outrageous exploits involved events during the Aroostook County drug wars that had occurred throughout his many years in the marijuana business.

In one instance, local pot dealers had been threatening friends of his. Infuriated, Bernard claimed to have burned their drug compound to the ground to send them a not so subtle message. According to him, the harassment promptly ended. On another occasion, competing pot growers had been trying to intimidate Max by shooting his cattle. Quietly getting the word out in the drug world that if the provocations continued someone was going to end up dead, he asserted there were no further incidents.

While neither of these stories can be confirmed, an observation by Mark Carney seems to aptly characterize Bernard, "He had excellent relationships with his friends, yet he could be unbelievably violent." It was common knowledge in the Aroostook County drug business that Bernard was not someone to mess with.

Boldness was an inherent part of other aspects of his life. While virtually all of his pot transactions were in cash to avoid providing evidence of criminal or tax violations, it was during this period that Bernard decided he needed a checking account for nonbusiness purposes. Inexplicably, he walked into the Northern National Bank to open an account. Cautious bank employees referred him to the branch manager. After a brief, candid discussion, the manager asked, "Why would we want to open an account with you with our money?" His application was denied. Bernard did not hold a grudge. He liked and respected the manager for his honesty.

* * *

By the 1990s, Bernard's pot growing activities had attracted the attention of those fighting the war on drugs. The U.S. Drug Enforcement Administration (DEA) had him in their cross-hairs. A cat and mouse game that would go on for years commenced. Agents would periodically stake out his property and unexpectedly drop by to interrogate him.

No one knew his land better than Bernard, and the former Viet Cong tracker had reconnaissance skills that put those possessed by the DEA agents to shame. Deciding to best them at their own game, Bernard acquired a DEA cap, jacket, and night vision goggles.

One night the DEA had eight agents stationed on a ridge overlooking his property. Using the covert deftness he'd learned and perfected in Vietnam, Bernard donned his DEA outfit and joined them during their surveillance. Unbeknownst to the agents, their targeted suspect spent most of the night in the woods in their midst, observing them. In fact, they were being intently scrutinized by a man who had the proven capacity to be a hardened killer. Had they been the Viet Cong, some if not all of the surreptitious investigators might have lost their lives that night. It was a very unproductive and potentially hazardous undertaking for the unsuspecting government spies.

After several failed attempts due to a lack of probable cause, the DEA obtained a warrant to search his house. Despite a painstaking effort, no incriminating evidence of marijuana growth or sales was found. While prison had been a very disagreeable experience for Bernard, the years he'd committed to the study of botany and devising schemes to conceal his plants had paid off quite handsomely.

While he was able to avoid any drug-related charges, agents did discover a .30-30 Winchester rifle in his possession during the search. Prohibited from owning a firearm as a convicted felon, he was jailed for a short time.

The humor of his seemingly endless clandestine contest with the drug officers of the DEA was not lost on Bernard. While shopping for a telephone in Walmart, he bumped into the manager, who was an old friend. Finishing a good-natured conversation, Bernard caustically remarked, "Come out and visit me sometime. The only people who visit me are the FBI and DEA."

Acknowledging that he was a known pot smoker and grower, the Walmart manager liked Bernard and considered him a friend. Describing him as "brazen and brave," he further observed, "He was a small guy, but you instinctively knew, don't mess with him."

* * *

Although the DEA didn't have the apparent resources or capabilities to catch him, Bernard was much less successful avoiding clashes with local law enforcement. In August 1997, he was arrested for operating a motor vehicle under the influence of alcohol, driving with a suspended license and probation violations.

Given his lengthy history of vehicular

infractions, the sentence was a harsh one. Ordered to serve forty-five days in jail, pay a $1,000 fine and suffer an additional four years of license suspension for the operating under the influence of alcohol charge, the court was unsympathetic concerning his latest transgressions. He also received another forty-five day sentence for probation violations and seven days in jail for operating a motor vehicle after license suspension.

His drinking was spiraling out of control and having a negative impact on his pot business. Unable to remain sober when transacting sales, customers were frequently cheating him when making purchases. Belatedly, Bernard realized he had a problem.

Characteristically, Bernard quit drinking cold turkey. But not smoking pot, or growing it.

* * *

After an absence of almost fifteen years, his friend Kyle returned to the area again in 2002. Now married and having recently started a business in a nearby town, he drove to Westfield to visit Bernard. Kyle was astounded to find him sober and romantically involved.

As they walked the pot fields together, Bernard observed that getting "clean" had given him a new lease on life. The previous year had been his most profitable pot season ever with sales approximating $250,000. His girl-friend was pregnant and he had built her a new home. The ramshackle hut, which had mysteriously burned, and the wild, night-long parties were things of the past. Expressing optimism about the future, life appeared to be taking a positive turn for him.

However, Bernard was not without problems. His pregnant girlfriend was more than thirty-five years his junior. That presented a multitude of difficult issues for Bernard. Concerned that she was the daughter of one of his high school classmates, he was worried about how to address their relationship with his old friend. Simply keeping pace with a twenty-year-old and meeting her sexual and emotional needs was daunting. Raising a child at his age also presented an intimidating challenge.

Undeterred, Bernard continued to have a ready smile and an ever-present twinkle in his eye.

• 24 •

Passing

"At the end of his life, his health failed badly. Looked like he'd been dragged through a key hole."
—Mark Carney, friend

Bernard's life journey ended prematurely on a beautiful, warm summer day when he died of a massive heart attack in a Presque Isle hospital on July 5, 2003. He died close to where he'd been born a little more than fifty-six years earlier.

It was an anonymous passing for the former war hero, bank robber, and international fugitive. His obituary was little more than a simple death announcement.

There was no newspaper or television coverage. Forgotten by the media that had followed and enthusiastically disclosed his valor and misdeeds, no one reported on his remarkable war time accomplishments, his almost unbelievable escape after the robbery, and the exploits and excesses he experienced in California, Europe, and North Africa. No mention was made of the many close friends he'd made during his travels through life or the combat buddies whose lives he'd saved and heroics shared. The many narrow escapes while being pursued by a determined international law enforcement community and the numerous loves he'd had and lost also went unreported.

However, the story of his deeds and misdeeds live on in the memories of his many loyal friends who still remember him with amazement four decades later. They recall a poor kid who had nothing, went to war, became a hero, returned with more than his share of baggage, and took on the world. And, for a brief period of time, he won the battle against staggering odds. Even after imprisonment, he refused to play by society's rules. In short, he never surrendered in Vietnam and seldom did in life.

Perhaps his final thoughts were of a dangerous assignment as a tunnel rat or his improbable escape after robbing the bank. Or, maybe he was thinking of the hardscrabble days of his youth. More likely, he was considering the botanical needs of his current marijuana crop or the weighty prospects of raising an infant with a very young wife. Of that, we'll never know.

Whatever he was, good, bad, ordinary or extraordinary, whatever reasons motivated him to do the things he did—selfishness, deep psychological issues, dysfunctional childhood, posttraumatic stress disorder, greed or hidden insecurities—he did them with an unusual flair for life that intrigued and astonished those who knew him. He had a lot more courage and a lot less fear than most of us who travel the road of life.

Epilogue

Who was Bernard Patterson is a question I've pondered many times. He could be ruthless and merciless with those he considered his enemies, yet generous and protective of his friends. While he often used his friends and lovers for self-serving purposes, most retained a lifelong loyalty and affection for him. He was callous with the women in his life and often sexually aggressive; however he could be thoughtful, considerate and romantic. He always maintained a tough outer image yet some who knew him intimately attest that he had a vulnerable side to his personality. He could be uncommonly greedy, robbing a bank, burglarizing his friend's uncle, embracing the black market in Vietnam and illegally running a lucrative pot farm for most of his adult life; yet he was unceasingly generous with friends and sometimes people he didn't even know. Extremely hard working when legitimately employed, he spent most of his last twenty-five years illicitly growing marijuana instead. When posttraumatic stress disorder (PTSD) was identified as a common affliction of Vietnam combat veterans, Bernard adamantly denied having any such problems. However, a professional counselor with a vast amount of experience with PTSD patients asserts that he exhibited classic behavior and symptoms. So, who was Bernard? After almost two years of researching him, I don't have a firm answer to the question. He was enigmatic, unpredictable and a man of many contradictions.

I regret having never met him. He died before I even seriously considered writing professionally. The dozens of people interviewed who knew him have been my window into his life and persona. Without their help and guidance, his story couldn't have been told.

Much of Bernard's narrative is more than forty years old. Many of the players involved in his life at that time have passed away and others have declined to share their knowledge and experiences. In some instances, time has distorted the recollections of those who have shared their memories. When possible, I have tried to reconcile the differences of conflicting recollections. However, in several instances, I have arbitrarily chosen the option that seemed most credible.

There are many aspects of the robbery, escape and his subsequent escapades where the only information available is what Bernard related to friends and during the interview with Ronald Bean. To the extent possible, I have attempted to corroborate his story. However, when in doubt or lacking other information, it's his story as he related it.

Acknowledgments

I am deeply indebted to many people who assisted me with this endeavor. Several sources have chosen to remain anonymous but their contributions were no less valuable.

Brian Blanchard shared many memories and chauffeured me around the Mars Hill area. Mark Carney shared many memories. Suzanne Cole provided library research guidance. Stuart Craig offered recollections from the night of the robbery. Harry Donovan shared memories. Launa Donovan provided very helpful and detailed recollections of the robbery. Larry Donovan shared memories. Wayne Donovan shared memories. Brent Elwell provided valued information on prison life. Brian Feuler with the *Bangor Daily News* was very helpful authorizing the use of an old photo of Bernard. Fay Fitzherbert shared many details surrounding the robbery. Riitta Fortier provided helpful research. Allen Gaskell offered his expertise regarding PTSD. Duane Grass shared memories and details of the fire before the robbery. Peter King shared memories. Normand McPherson shared memories. Martha Lawrence provided information on Northern National Bank procedures and shared memories. Harry Orser shared memories. Mars Hill Town Manager Karin Petrin cordially offered access to the Town Office which was formerly Northern National Bank. Doug Pierce shared many memories. Mark Putnam graciously provided access to the *Star Herald* archives. Ronald Sargent shared memories. Photographer Daryn Slover authorized the use of a photo he shot. Editorial Director Michael Steere was enthusiastic and supportive of the book proposal. Lifelong friend Ed Strollo did a first read of the manuscript and offered valued advice. Dottie Wheeler shared her memories of the night of the robbery and phone calls between Bernard and her late husband Edgar.

My sons Eric and Adam offered encouragement and support throughout and my wife, Nancy, was very supportive and always available with much needed computer assistance.

Sources

Several sources who were friends or intimates of Bernard have chosen to remain anonymous. Their assistance in helping to construct Bernard's story have been invaluable and much appreciated. I have made every effort to protect their confidentiality. However, except in instances where disclosing the confidential information provided might indicate who the source was, I have indicated that an anonymous source offered the information related to that topic or event.

Three of the *Bangor Daily News* articles (October 25, 1973; October 26, 1973; and October 27 and 28, 1973) were the result of a prison interview with Bernard conducted by Ronald T. Bean and then written in collaboration with *Bangor Daily News* staff writer John S. Day.

CHAPTER 1, REFLECTIONS

- Quotes by William Yersa and a former school teacher: *Bangor Daily News* 9/24/72
- Details of Bernard's childhood: Doug Pierce,

Brian Blanchard, Larry Donovan, Duane Grass, Mark Carney and anonymous sources
- Description of working with Bernard in the potato houses: Larry Donovan
- Bernard's expression of disappointment with the absence of his mother and being farmed out to family members and description of families picking potatoes: anonymous source
- Ola Orser's comments on Bernard's visits to Northern National Bank prior to the robbery: Harry Orser
- Details of experiences in Vietnam: Brian Blanchard, Doug Pierce and anonymous sources
- Information about black market activities: Doug Pierce, Mark Carney and anonymous sources
- Information on the tunnels of Cu Chi and tunnel rats, descriptions of tunnels, Bob Hope entertainment incident, underground tank and tunnel hazards: *The Tunnels of Cu Chi*, Tom Mangold and John Penycate
- Comments regarding Bernard's desire that a book be written or movie produced: Peter King
- Information on combat awards: *Bangor Daily News* 12/6/73

CHAPTER 2, RETURN HOME

- Pursuit of high school diploma: *Bangor Daily News* 12/3/71
- Details of Al's Diner robbery: *Bangor Daily News* 12/4/71 & 12/5/71
- Smith's Truck Stop robbery: *Bangor Daily News* 9/4/72 and anonymous source
- Information on hooches and life in Vietnam: *The Tunnels of Cu Chi*, Tom Mangold and John Penycat, Peter King, Brian Blanchard and Doug Pierce
- Black market activities: Mark Carney, Doug Pierce and anonymous sources
- Life while home on leave between tours in Vietnam: Mark Carney, Brian Blanchard, Doug Pierce and anonymous source
- Corvette stories: Brian Blanchard, Mark Carney, Doug Pierce, Wayne Donovan and anonymous source
- Speculation regarding mental instability being the basis for denial of a fourth tour in Vietnam: Mark Carney, Doug Pierce and anonymous source
- Lifestyle when Bernard returned from Vietnam after separation from the military: Mark Carney, Brian Blanchard, Doug Pierce and anonymous source
- Conviction of Gary Mahaney and David

Bradbury: Kennebec County Superior Court records

- Disillusionment with Veteran's Administration: Peter King
- Loan from Mark Carney: Mark Carney
- Regular visits to Northern National Bank before robbery: Harry Orser, Martha Lawrence and Wayne Donovan
- Loan from Brian Blanchard: Brian Blanchard
- Fire on November 5, 1971: *Bangor Daily News* 10/25/73, Duane Grass and Fay Fitzherbert

CHAPTER 3, THE ROBBERY

- Details of the robbery: *Bangor Daily News* 11/15/71 &10/25/73, Harry Orser, Ronald Sargent, and Launa Donovan
- Bernard carried an unloaded gun: *Bangor Daily News* 12/6/72
- Largest bank robbery in Maine history: *Bangor Daily News* 11/21/71
- Phone conversations regarding robbery: Dottie Wheeler
- Ella Bartley's activities during the robbery: *Bangor Daily News* 10/25/73 & 11/15/71 and Launa Donovan
- Information regarding the November 5, 1971 fire: Duane Grass and Fay Fitzherbert

CHAPTER 4, THE SEARCH

CHAPTER 5, THE ESCAPE

- Description of foiled kayak attempt, escape through potato fields, Deputy Wheeler search, encounter with dead bear, hiding out on Mars Hill Mountain, burying $17,000, awoken by animal, return to Mars Hill and meeting Canadian drug dealers: *Bangor Daily News* 10/25/73 & 10/26/73
- Motorcycling on Mars Hill Mountain roads: Anonymous
- Hiding out on backside of Mars Hill Mountain, kayaking down Prestile Stream, hiking across snowy potato fields to Mars Hill Mountain, activities after he returned to Mars Hill and time in Presque Isle: Mark Carney

CHAPTER 6, THE INVESTIGATION

- Bernard riding Deputy Wheeler's horses: Dottie Wheeler
- Stopping the gray Oldsmobile and searching cabin and source of smoke on Mars Hill Mountain: Fay Fitzherbert
- Results of post-robbery internal bank audit: Martha Lawrence
- Phone calls to Aroostook Health Center: *Bangor Daily News* 11/15/71

- Fire investigation: Duane Grass and Fay Fitzherbert
- Cloak of secrecy surrounding the investigation: *Star Herald* 11/17/71
- Bernard had several romantic interests in Mars Hill area and girlfriend in Bangor: *Bangor Daily News* 9/4/72
- Announcement of warrant for arrest: *Bangor Daily News* 12/3/71
- State Grand Jury indictment for Al's Diner burglary: *Bangor Daily News* 12/4/71 & 12/5/71
- Post-robbery quotes recalling Bernard as a good kid: *Bangor Daily News* 12/13/71
- January Federal Grand Jury hearing: *Star Herald* 1/19/72

CHAPTER 7, TRANS AMERICA

- Left Maine in a cloud of marijuana smoke, traveled with two Canadian dope pushers to Bradley Field Connecticut, flew to Los Angeles via Houston, searched for army buddies, located Bruce at UCLA Law School and planned Swiss ski trip: *Bangor Daily News* 10/26/73
- Rules and life as a tunnel rat: *The Tunnels of Cu Chi*, Tom Mangold and John Penycate

CHAPTER 8, TRANSFORMATION

- Federal court evidence shows Bernard purchased the passport of Robert Peter Inman: *Bangor Daily News* 12/6/72
- Details of Charlotte Dunn murder and subsequent criminal proceedings against Robert P. Inman: Supreme Judicial Court of Maine
- Purchase of Robert Peter Inman's passport, police holding another Peter Inman in Bangor, Maine: *Bangor Daily News* 10/26/73

CHAPTER 9, TRANS ATLANTIC

- Flew from LA to Paris, suitcases and stockings stuffed with money, walked through customs without incident, money slipping from Dingo boots: *Bangor Daily News* 10/26/73
- Met Maggie: *Bangor Daily News* 10/27/73 & 10/28/73
- Details of the U.S. Attorney warrant for arrest: *Bangor Daily News* 12/ 4/71 & 12/5/71

CHAPTER 10, SWISS RATS

- Spent sometimes as much as $1,200 a day, stayed at Hotel de la Paix, dressed in corduroy jeans and Dingo boots on arrival, ate at most expensive restaurants including Auberge de la Mere Royaume, discovered Genevois cooking and addicted to fondue Bourguignonne, dined at Perle du Lac and Café Mozart, addiction to vintage wines, spent 740 francs for bottle of Chateau Lafite and spent $4,000 in four days on food and drink: *Bangor Daily News* 10/26/73

CHAPTER 11, LAST OF THE RATS

- Moved to Villars-sur-Ollon, traveled by limousine, checked into Palace Hotel, started skiing Bretaye, Bruce developed serious cold and departed to California, met two Dutch girls and alone again: *Bangor Daily News* 10/26/73

CHAPTER 12, DECADENT RAT

- Two Dutch girls joined him in the chalet, followed by two from England and then two from Canada; three men, an Italian, Austrian and Dutchman followed them. Fondue dinners at Hotel Central, New Year's Eve party and lavish spending, installed stereo system in chalet, commissioned Lombard to make silver bracelet and jade ring, another expensive clothes shopping spree, feasted on Scotch smoked salmon and lobsters, ate raclette on top of the mountain, purchased half interest in restaurant in Malaga, Spain and extravagant living attracted attention of Swiss authorities: *Bangor Daily News* 10/26/73

- Rented chalet from landlord who was an influential Swiss banker, met motorcyclist from Toronto, Ontario, wooed Maggie in Switzerland: *Bangor Daily News* 10/27/73 & 10/28/73
- Story about blowing up hooch in Vietnam and transfer to Texas: anonymous source

CHAPTER 13, HOMESICK

- Horseback riding, phone conversations and friendship with Deputy Wheeler: Dottie Wheeler
- Phone call to Brian Blanchard and follow-up with FBI: Brian Blanchard
- Transcript of phone conversation with Deputy Wheeler, Swiss authorities interested in

wild spending, sent Paris original to Maine sweetheart: *Bangor Daily News* 10/27/73 & 10/28/73

CHAPTER 14, CORNERED RAT

- Swiss police suspicious, continued to throw lavish parties, authorities discovered non-payment of taxation du jour, Bernard ordered to police station, showed up at 3:00 instead of 9:00 and forgot passport, summoned a second time and claimed passport misplaced, Swiss Police demanded photo, sent photo to the United States but it got lost in bureaucratic channels, police decided to declare him undesirable, brought influential Swiss banker and landlord who objected to harassment and police backed down, German Swiss friend informed Bernard of wanted photo in Zurich, packed bags and flew to Maggie in England, two Interpol agents knocked on door a half hour after he left: *Bangor Daily News* 10/27/73 & 10/28/73

CHAPTER 15, ROYAL WELCOME

- Maggie lived in Staines, met her father who was a doctor, she showed Bernard around southern England including Piccadilly Square, father diagnosed Bernard with alcohol poisoning, Maggie returned to work as a stewardess and Bernard was very bored: *Bangor Daily News* 10/27/73 & 10/28/73

CHAPTER 16, ROBIN RAT?

- Canoe trip on Allagash: Anonymous
- Slipped $1,000 into purse of woman separated from daughter, purposely lost $2,000 in crap game to ski instructor who had run over a girl and couldn't afford her hospital expenses, gave two Irish girls the money to fly home, contemplated establishing an orphanage with one of his girlfriends in Switzerland: *Bangor Daily News* 10/26/73
- Repayment of loan to Brian Blanchard: Brian Blanchard

CHAPTER 17, A GREEK TRAGEDY

- Bumped into Canadian friend in England, two decided to drink and womanize their way across the continent, objective was Ios in Greece, bought two motorcycles (Triumph 650 and Trophy 500), ferried to Calais, biked through France, Switzerland and Yugoslavia, Patterson denied entry to Greece because of phony passport, border guards let him go, Canadian left him alone: *Bangor Daily News* 10/27/73 & 10/28/73

- Gambling addiction: anonymous source

CHAPTER 18, DESERT RAT

- Collected ears of his kills in Vietnam: anonymous source
- Traveled through Italy to Houmt Souk in Tunisia, bought a camel for $200 and galloped into sand dunes of Sahara alone, got lost for two and half days eventually traveling in circles, camel took control and returned to stable, headed back to England: *Bangor Daily News* 10/27/73 & 10/28/73

CHAPTER 19, WHEN IRISH EYES ARE SMILING

- Hard partying in Isle of Jersey, identification problems: Mark Carney
- Met with Doug Pierce at Camp Eagle Vietnam while stationed with 101st Airborne and selling pot to friend: Doug Pierce
- Traveled to Isle of Jersey, struck up friendship with two Irish ladies, joined them at hut, got into brawl with fisherman who beat the

daylights out of him for sleeping with his wife and sister: *Bangor Daily News* 10/27/73 & 10/28/73, Anonymous source

CHAPTER 20, RAT TRAP

- Elaborate manhunt conducted on Isle of Jersey: *Bangor Daily News* 11/21/72
- Apprehended by Scotland Yard agents on June 9, 1972. Was carrying 5000 Swiss francs: *Bangor Daily News* 10/11/72
- Bernard quote and details of arrest: *Bangor Daily News* 10/26/73
- Unique ability to blend into situations, particularly in Vietnam: Doug Pierce and anonymous source

CHAPTER 21, SHOW ME THE MONEY

- Extradition order, accompanied by Guy Patterson to the United States, arrival in New York, appearance before U.S. Magistrate, remanded to Maine, appearance before Magistrate Keith, innocent plea, additional Aroostook County charges and U.S. Attorney Mills statement that there was no information on missing money: *Bangor Daily News* 10/11/72
- Changed plea, scheduled 12/5/72 hearing: *Bangor Daily News* 11/21/72

- Sentencing, arrival at court, details of 12/5/72 hearing, details of recovery of money in Mars Hill, incarceration in Pentonville Prison awaiting extradition: *Bangor Daily News* 2/6/72
- Questioning by Judge Gignoux, quotes by Attorney Zendzian, beating by inmates in Penobscot County Jail, additional sentencing information and transfer to Lewisburg Federal Penitentiary: *Bangor Daily News* 10/26/73
- Information regarding observations of federal marshal during return flight: Mark Carney

CHAPTER 22, SCARED RAT

- Details of experiences in prison, Bernard quotes, description of Ruthanne and her employment with UMPI: Mark Carney
- Description of typical prison life: Brent Elwell
- Information on *Bangor Daily News* interviews: *Bangor Daily News* 10/25/73, 10/26/73, 10/27/73 & 10/28/73
- Observations on marijuana botanic skills and starting pot farm: anonymous Source
- Real estate acquisition: Aroostook County Registry of Deeds
- Feigned nervous breakdown and early release: Wayne Donovan
- Transfer to Portland Halfway House: anonymous Source

CHAPTER 23, LIVING THE HIGH LIFE

- Deputy Wheeler stopped Bernard for speeding: Dottie Wheeler
- Information on pot growing, relationship with pot dealer, heavy beer drinking, drug war stories, DEA story, drinking problem, getting sober, building new home, girlfriend pregnant and quote at heading: anonymous source
- Visit, camping in Westfield, parties and drinking problem: Doug Pierce
- UMPI information, relationship with Ruthanne and discussions with Bernard: Mark Carney
- National Guard story: anonymous source
- Hauling organic wheat story: Duane Grass
- Northern National Bank story, DEA quote and Walmart story: anonymous source
- Vehicle violations: *Bangor Daily News* 8/25/97
- Working on Houlton border crossing and firearm conviction: Harry Donovan
- Theft of fertilizer: anonymous source

CHAPTER 24, PASSING

- Obituary: Maine Public Library and *Bangor Daily News* 7/8/03

About Names

For a variety of reasons, I have chosen to use some fictitious names or partial names. Any similarity to anyone having those names is purely coincidental. The names identified below were fictitious.

CHAPTER 7, TRANS AMERICA

- Pierre, Richard, Emilio Gonzales and Tom Maury
- Bernard identified his UCLA Vietnam buddy as Bruce but the last name Hakala is fictitious

CHAPTER 8, TRANSFORMATION

- Lunar Eclipse and Angela Liebowitz

CHAPTER 9, TRANS ATLANTIC

- Bernard identified Maggie as his English stewardess love interest but the name Margaret Ward is fictitious

CHAPTER 10, SWISS RATS

- Mia

CHAPTER 11, LAST OF THE RATS

- Sophie and Lotte

Center Point Large Print
600 Brooks Road / PO Box 1
Thorndike, ME 04986-0001 USA

(207) 568-3717

US & Canada:
1 800 929-9108
www.centerpointlargeprint.com